Agape Light Ministries

Walking in the Light

Carol Ann Caster

Walking in the Light
by Carol Ann Caster

Printed in the United States of America

ISBN 978-1-60791-328-3

www.xulonpress.com

FOREWORD

I count it a great privilege to have been afforded the opportunity to read many pieces that Minister Carol Ann Caster has written. I have also had the great opportunity to listen to her radio broadcasts. There is no doubt that her relationship with the Holy Spirit is active and real. I can attest to the fruit in her life of ministry and veracity to the Word is unmistakable.

Carol Ann has been a willing servant to the Body of Christ and has been a tremendous blessing both to me personally and also to the ministry of 2 Timothy 4:5 while she was acting Director for the Southern United States. I whole heartedly believe that it was by divine appointment that the Holy Spirit led her into a ministry relationship with us and through that a friendship.

Without the Holy Spirit we can ultimately accomplish nothing that has eternal value. It is this love and relationship with the Holy Spirit that motivates Carol Ann. You can read it in her writings, hear it in her speaking and feel the compassion in her conversation. It is the compassion and desire to fulfill the Great Commission that has her words always pointing back to the Lord Jesus Christ.

Again I was blessed and comforted as I read "Walking in the Light" as the Spirit of God began to unfold the truth from His Word through the writing of Carol Ann. It

has been a true privilege to receive this book for my own spiritual enrichment and I have no doubt that countless others will also be enriched and blessed as they encounter the Holy Spirit through this inspired book.

Thank you Carol Ann for all that you do.

In His service,

Overseer Scott Whitwam
2 Timothy 4:5

Spring's Hope

One day I came to seek my Lord,
And knelt on bended knee,
I cried my Savior, King, my All
Please hear my needful plea.

So many struggles surround me
And I am downcast in my soul.
Then He said, have faith My child,
I will make you whole.

In the winters of your difficulties,
Where your natural eye can't see,
The seeds of faith are growing
As you place your trust in Me.

And as you hope for things unseen,
My Word will prosper there,
To bring about the very thing
That you have sought in prayer.

For to those who will believe in Me,
And walk by faith, not sight,
Will I manifest My Presence
As the day breaks forth from night.

So I lifted up my head with joy,
And my heart began to sing ...
Praises to my Savior, God,
My All in All, my King!

Why were you downcast oh my soul?
His Word does always bring,
From any barren place or trial,
The Hope and Life of Spring.

"Carol Ann"

TABLE OF CONTENTS

WALKING IN THE LIGHT PREFACE

It is with great awe and humility before the Living Word that this devotional is presented. The messages it holds are offered only as precious nuggets from His treasure chest of Truth. There is so much more that the fullness of His Word holds. In fact, an eternity's worth. Therefore, it is my heartfelt hope that as you read this book, you will not only be encouraged and enriched but that you will be filled with a hunger for more of HIM. Any writing that God's vessel is anointed to produce should not only echo His inerrant Word, but also point the reader back to all He has spoken in His Holy Testaments that are held in His Bible.

I will also mention that this work was prophesied many years before it actually came to pass and was then confirmed just recently. There were two saints in particular who would encourage me to not shrink back from writing the "Agape Light Newsletter" from which these devotionals have been taken. Therefore, "Walking in the Light" has become a reality only because of His Grace and the vessels He ordained to participate in its completion. Because we are still on earth there are natural things that play a part in God's spiritual purposes. This book

could not have been published without that intervention taking place. In addition to the spiritual encouragement that was provided, Jehovah-Jireh touched the hearts of a small number of His vessels who have generously blessed Agape Light Ministries with financial gifts. Certain ones continue sacrificially to do so and I would delight to honor them by mentioning them by name. However, I was quickened in my spirit that by remaining anonymous their blessing from our Father will be even greater. As you read this you know who you are; and more importantly He knows. Thank you so very much for your obedience and willingness to be used by Him in this way. Together we serve our Master Jesus in this ministry effort.

To my Husband Paul, who is one with me in all that our God is purposing in this glorious journey, I say thank you especially. You are the vessel the Lord raised up in administrative anointing to make this book a reality. Through you the Lord breathed on the embers of a dream He gave me long ago. In my heart the vision had virtually died and I no longer had the desire to publish a book. But then I suppose that is when we are ready to be used by our God. When we have come to the end of our self, and the greatest desire of our heart is only for Him, that is the time He can begin to show forth His Glory in and through us. At this point, He will bring about those things He has purposed before the foundation of the world and all praise becomes His alone.

Finally to my wonderful Mother and Dad, my treasured children and their mates, and my beautiful brothers and sisters and their families.... I love you all so very much and thank our God with all my heart for you!

In closing, I give the Lord ALL HONOR, GLORY AND PRAISE FOREVER! FOR HE IS FOREVER WORTHY! The time is short and my spirit bears witness to His soon Return. As He prepares His Bride in Holiness,

He is calling us to walk more fully in the Power of His Word as the "*new creations*" we have become in our precious Savior, Jesus the Christ. Therefore, keep "Walking in the Light," and as always beloved.....Agape!

Carol Ann

Devotion One

"ENCOUNTERING THE LIGHT"

"And it came about that as I was on my way, approaching Damascus about noontime, a very bright light suddenly flashed from heaven all around me, and I fell to the ground and heard a voice saying to me, 'Saul, Saul, why are you persecuting Me?' And I answered, 'Who art Thou, Lord?' And He said to me, 'I am Jesus the Nazarene, whom you are persecuting.' And those who were with me beheld the light, to be sure, but did not understand the voice of the One who was speaking to me. And I said, 'What shall I do Lord?' And the Lord said to me, 'Arise and go on into Damascus; and there you will be told of all that has been appointed for you to do.' But since I could not see because of the brightness of that light, I was led by the hand by those who were with me, and came into Damascus. And a certain Ananias, a man who was devout by the standard of the Law, and well spoken of by all the Jews who lived there, came to me, and standing near said to me, 'Brother Saul, receive your sight!'

> ***And at that very time I looked up at him. And he said, 'The God of our fathers has appointed you to know His will, and to see the Righteous One, and to hear an utterance from His mouth. For you will be a witness for Him to all men of what you have seen and heard.'"*** **Acts 22:6-15**

What a marvelous account of Paul's encounter with the Living Word! In the previous verses of Acts Chapter 22, we are told that Paul had been seized in the temple and accused of preaching to all men everywhere against the Jews and the Law. In the passage above, we pick up where in his defense Paul begins to testify of his encounter with the Lord Jesus on the Damascus road. Chapter 9 of Acts goes into more detail as to why Paul happened to be in that particular place on that day. Before his conversion, he had been threatening the disciples of the Lord and had requested letters from the high priest that he intended to take to the synagogues at Damascus. Then if Paul found any people belonging to the Way, he could bring them bound to Jerusalem.

Paul had plans. He had purpose. He had zeal. He even had intellectual and religious information to support his cause. He was, after all, a diligent student of the Law. In all of this, however, Paul was missing the most vital necessity. Paul had yet to encounter the Light! (John 8:12)

Therefore, all of his actions produced only darkness, only death. But as he traveled that day – the day appointed for him before the foundations of the world – the Light came to him. It knocked him off the high horse of self-righteousness. It blinded him from all that he thought he could see with his natural eyes and understand with his own finite mind. All he saw now was Jesus! He had come face to face with Love! The course of Paul's life had been changed forever. When Love spoke, Paul knew he

had heard the voice of the One Who alone is Truth and his spiritual eyes were opened. The Light of God's Love would now lead the way, and Paul would forever follow.

Paul had been called, and he was chosen. The Light came, the Word spoke, Paul responded. Another Will had replaced his. Higher plans were on the horizon, and Paul's zeal had become sanctified. The Divine appointment for his life was revealed: *"The God of our fathers has appointed you to know His will, and to see the Righteous One, and to hear an utterance from His mouth. For you will be a witness for Him to all men of what you have seen and heard."* (Acts 22:14 & 15)

Blessed believer, in whom the Light dwells, what has He appointed you to? His Will has been made known to you by His Word. In John 6:39-40, Jesus declares: *"And this is the will of Him who sent Me, that of all that He has given Me I lose nothing, but raise it up on the last day. For this is the will of My Father, that everyone who beholds the Son and believes in Him, may have eternal life; and I Myself will raise him up on the last day."*

This wonderful Truth is now the very essence, the very Life within you. It is the Father's intention that you should walk in the Power of this reality, and be His servant in the capacity to which you are called in Him. The works are already prepared for you to walk in them (Eph. 2:10). Just surrender your will afresh and look to the Light. You will see Him, the Righteous One. And as your spiritual eyes behold His Glory, your natural eyes will be blinded from seeing anything but what He sees. And you will hear an utterance from His mouth (John 10:14, 15, 16). For you too are called to be a witness for Him to all men of what you have seen and heard. The Lord is there to lead and direct you. His Word is the Lamp to your feet - the Light to your path. (Ps. 119:105)

Therefore, be encouraged, beloved, and press on in confidence. The Lord is God, and He reigns Supreme! Amen!

Devotion Two

"TEST THE SPIRITS"

***"Beloved, do not believe every spirit, but test the spirits to see whether they are from God; because many false prophets have gone out into the world. By this you know the Spirit of God: every spirit that confesses that Jesus Christ has come in the flesh is from God; and every spirit that does not confess Jesus is not from God; and this is the spirit of the antichrist, of which you have heard that it is coming, and now it is already in the world. You are from God, little children, and have overcome them; because greater is He who is in you than he who is in the world. They are from the world; therefore they speak as from the world, and the world listens to them. We are from God; he who knows God listens to us; he who is not from God does not listen to us. By this we know the spirit of truth and the spirit of error."* 1 John 4:1-6**

This Light-filled passage has been given to us to keep us from being caught up in the web of great deception the enemy has woven upon this planet. In every dark

place, the Lord God has provided Light. We learn that: *"In the beginning God created the heavens and the earth. And the earth was formless and void, and darkness was over the face of the deep; and the Spirit of God was moving over the surface of the waters. Then God said, 'Let there be light;' and there was light. And God saw that the light was good; and God separated the light from the darkness."* (Gen. 1:1-4)

Darkness causes fear. Because what we cannot see we do not know, and we cannot be sure where we are going. Neither do we know what might be lurking about to harm us. Or worse, we may feel a false sense of safety with the darkness wrapped around us like a blanket, yet fear is never far away. But there is no darkness at all in the Father of Lights – not even a variation or shifting of shadow; and every perfect gift is from Him above (James 1:17). His Light has come to show the way into the safety of His Love and to expose every dark place that holds danger and falsehood.

Darkness and Light can have no fellowship. They have been forever separated by the Father of Lights. The Light brings forth Life and Truth; while darkness breeds only death and deceit. Therefore, wherever Light is found the Living God and all the fullness of His blessings will be manifested. But if we have entered a dark place, it is certain that the enemy's schemes of deception and destruction are at work. So then in order to be kept in the safeguard of the Light of His Truth, we are exhorted to not "*believe*" every spirit.

To understand this directive more fully we are taught that the English word "*believe*" comes from the Greek word "*pisteuo*," meaning "*to have faith in or entrust to.*" If we believe any other spirit than the Holy Spirit we are entrusting our faith to the realm of Satan's darkness and deception. Therefore we are called to "*test*" the spirits to

see whether or not they are from God. The Greek word for "*test*" is "*dokimazo*" and means: *"to analyze, examine, approve, as you would a legal document."*

By His Word the Lord God makes very certain how we will know that which is from the Holy Spirit and that which is of the devil. "*By this you know the Spirit of God: every spirit that confesses that Jesus Christ has come in the flesh is from God; and every spirit that does not confess Jesus is not from God, and is the spirit of the antichrist*" (1 John 4:2-3). Here, the Greek word for "*confess*" is "*homologeo*" which means "*to assent, acknowledge, i.e. as in covenant.*"

This holds a stronger meaning than just mentally agreeing or saying that Jesus Christ has come in the flesh, for even the demons believe and shudder (James 2:19). In Isaiah 29:13-14, the Lord declares: "*Because this people draw near with their words and honor Me with their lip service, but they remove their hearts far from Me, and their reverence for Me consists of tradition learned by rote, therefore behold, I will once again deal marvelously with this people, wondrously marvelous; and the wisdom of their wise men shall perish, and the discernment of their discerning men shall be concealed.*" The Hebrew word for "*marvelously*" in this passage is "*pala*" and means in part "*to deal with in a hard and astonishing way: to be separate from.*" God cannot be one with those whose hearts have not been circumcised and surrendered fully to Him.

Therefore, we see that more is required than mere lip service in man's confession of Jesus. And the yielding of mankind to a system of values and better behavior does not indicate true submission to the Lord either. Man can act out a superficial goodness so that things will be more comfortable for him on this planet, while in his heart he remains in complete rebellion to God and His Word. This charade will still leave him completely separated from

the Father Who loves humanity so much that He gave His Own Son to reconcile the world back to Himself. True reconciliation requires more than religious platitudes. It is only realized by genuine repentance from the heart and Covenant with God.

To have Covenant with the Living God is to be married to Him and belong completely and faithfully to Him alone. No other loves. No one you desire but Him. It is a Covenant that has been sealed by the Blood of Jesus and results in a complete conversion to a Saving Faith and Eternal Life in Him. It is complete agreement with His Word. Nothing added, nothing taken away. No darkness or confusion, only pure Truth and pure Light. And we have been given the Safeguard Who now lives within the hearts of those who have been "*born again.*" His Name is Holy Spirit, and "*greater is He who is in us than he who is in the world*" (I John 4:4). He is our Helper given to lead us into all Truth (John 16:13); and the One Who calls to those who have yet to encounter the True Light. Darkness must flee in the Light of His scrutiny; for His Holy Fire will burn away all falsehood and deception. He has forever conquered the evil one who disguises himself as an angel of light (2 Cor. 11:14), and exposes him by the Truth of His Word!

Oh beloved, how Awesome and Great is the Lord our God! How wonderful and perfect is His Love for us! Let us press on as lovers of His Truth and continue to worship Him in that Truth and by His Spirit. Amen!

Devotion Three

"GREATER WORKS"

"Truly, truly, I say to you, he who believes in Me, the works that I do shall he do also; and greater works than these shall he do; because I go to the Father. And whatever you ask in My name that will I do, that the Father may be glorified in the Son. If you ask Me anything in My name, I will do it. If you love Me, you will keep My commandments. And I will ask the Father, and He will give you another Helper, that He may be with you forever; that is the Spirit of truth whom the world cannot receive, because it does not behold Him or know Him, but you know Him because He abides with you, and will be in you. I will not leave you as orphans; I will come to you. After a little while the world will behold Me no more; but you will behold Me; because I live, you shall live also." **John 14:12-19**

The Word, the Promise, the Life! Lord Jesus is speaking to our hearts today even as He spoke these very words some 2000 years ago; for the Word of our God stands forever (Is. 40:8). And in light of this powerful

Truth, I cry out with the father who came to Jesus to heal his son possessed with a spirit that made him mute, "*I do believe; help my unbelief.*"

It is at the point of believing in the Lord Jesus that Divine activity is manifested. Even the very act of believing itself and the "*works*" that follow are evidence of the Presence of Holy Spirit, our Helper. The Greek word for "*works*" in the John 14:12-19 passage is "*ergon.*" It means: "*labor enjoined by and done for Christ as in spreading His Gospel.*"

In the Book of John, Chapter 6, verses 27-29, we read the instructional words of Jesus as He ministers to the multitude: "*Do not work for the food which perishes, but for the food which endures to eternal life, which the Son of Man shall give to you, for on Him the Father, even God, has set His seal.*" In response, the people who were standing there said: "*What shall we do, that we may work the works of God?*" The Lord then responded: "*This is the work of God, that you believe in Him whom He has sent.*"

Belief and the works of God go hand in hand; for it is by faith in His finished work on the Cross that we move in the flow of those things He has purposed to accomplish in and through us as His vessels. These Divine works were prepared before the foundation of the world and we are now equipped in Him to walk out their fulfillment. (Eph. 2:10)

As His legitimate children, He now abides in us by His Holy Spirit and we abide in Him by His Word. In this Sacred Abode His "*works*" are revealed. Our belief in all He has spoken creates the atmosphere in which His Promises are manifested in His Glorious signs and wonders. (Acts 2:43, 5:12, 6:8)

But the truly "*greater works*" are realized in the reality that a company of people who have not seen Him, believe in and love Him (1 Peter 1:8). He has gone to the Father,

but His Spirit still dwells among us and bears witness to the Truth. We can now "*ask*" anything according to His Word and He will do all He has promised because of His faithfulness and the integrity of His "*Name*" which is all Authority.

In our labor of love to Him we are kept in His Sabbath Rest, for it is all His work. He, therefore, receives all the Glory! We are merely the vessels through whom He is performing His Will. This eternal work produces eternal food. Jesus is the True Bread out of Heaven that feeds and nourishes the hungry soul. The one who has been made alive and strengthened by this Heavenly Manna now loves even as he has been loved, and keeping His Commandments is not burdensome. The Helper is forever with us to comfort, strengthen and equip us in all things.

In Deuteronomy 30:11 it is written: "*For this commandment which I command you today is not too difficult for you, nor is it out of reach. It is not in heaven, that you should say, 'Who will go up to heaven for us to get it for us and make us hear it, that we may observe it?' Nor is it beyond the sea, that you should say, 'Who will cross the sea for us to get it for us and make us hear it, that we may observe it?' But the word is very near you, in your mouth and in your heart, that you may observe it.'* " Heavenly food in eternal supply has been given to us so that we will never be hungry or find our hearts in want. It will forever strengthen us to walk in obedience and faithfulness to His Name. Praise God forever!

In closing, it is noteworthy to observe that so often our Savior begins His statements with the word "*truly*" and repeats it for added emphasis. It is the Greek word "*amen*" which means "*trustworthy.*" From the start, He assures us that the words that follow are sure and true, and in them we are to put our complete trust. We usually

say "*amen*" at the end of a prayer or especially after His declarations to us, indicating our agreement with what He has said. We are in effect saying "*it is so.*" He puts His "*amen*" at the beginning of His declarations, indicating that it has already been settled, whether we agree or not. *"Forever, O Lord, Thy Word is settled in heaven."* (Ps. 119:89)

Oh blessed child of God, may we believe more and more! And in the believing, may His "*works*" increase among us, as the time of His Coming draws nearer with each day. We have not been left as orphans; He will come for us.

In the meantime, if you become weak or weary in the waiting, there is an ample supply of "*Heavenly Bread*" to nourish and strengthen you. Believe! Ask! Receive!

The storehouses of Heaven await you, and you know the Way. Amen

Devotion Four

"IT IS FINISHED"

"For as the rain and the snow come down from heaven, and do not return there without watering the earth, and making it bear and sprout, and furnishing seed to the sower and bread to the eater; so shall my Word be which goes forth from My mouth; it shall not return to Me empty, without accomplishing what I desire, and without succeeding in the matter for which I sent it." **Isaiah 55:10-11**

"In the beginning was the Word, and the Word was with God, and the Word was God. He was in the beginning with God. All things came into being by Him, and apart from Him nothing came into being that has come into being. In Him was life, and the life was the light of men." **John 1:1-3**

"And the Word became flesh, and dwelt among us, and we beheld His glory, glory as of the only begotten from the Father, full of grace and truth." **John 1:14**

***Jesus said to them, "My food is to do the will of Him who sent Me, and to accomplish His work."* John 4:34**

***"It is finished."* John 19:30**

Within these awesome Scriptures, we see the progression of God's Prophetic Promises becoming reality in Jesus Christ the Living Word. The Word was sent and the Word came. Salvation's Covenant was made, ratified and sealed.

In three Dunamis empowered words, Jesus the Messiah acknowledged this Covenant reality: "IT IS FINISHED!" (Emphasis mine) John 19:30 records these words of Jesus as He bowed His head, and gave up His spirit to the Father. He had obediently fulfilled to perfection all the Father had sent Him to do. The enemy had been defeated by the shed Blood of the Spotless Lamb of God!

In confirmation, the Greek word for "*finished*" in this passage is "*teleo*," which means "*accomplished.*" Jesus was not returning to His Father empty-handed. He had succeeded in the matter for which He had come. The Living Water had been poured out for sinful man and produced a fertile growing place. The Word – God's Holy Seed - was then planted as a living sacrifice for us. *"Truly, truly, I say to you, unless a grain of wheat falls into the earth and dies, it remains by itself alone; but if it dies, it bears much fruit."* (John 12:24)

In the winter of His death was hidden the spring of His Glorious Resurrection! And what an abundant harvest has been produced and is still being produced in the soil of the hearts of those who would believe and receive so great a Salvation!

We are taught in Hebrews 4:12: "*For the Word of God is living and active and sharper than any two-edged sword, and piercing as far as the division of soul and spirit, of both joints and marrow, and able to judge the thoughts and intentions of the heart.*"

Jesus Christ is the Living Word! He is Alive! He is Active! He is still succeeding in the matter for which the Father sent Him. He is the Judge over every speculation and lofty thing raised up against the true knowledge of God, and the One Who enables us to take every thought captive in obedience to Him (2 Cor. 10:5).

In the span of time on this planet, words that can almost not be numbered have been spoken and recorded. Many of them have greatly influenced us and even stirred our emotions or changed the pattern of how we do things down here. But beloved brethren, only One Word is Living! Only One has the Power to SAVE, HEAL, DELIVER, and REDEEM! May the Lord keep this knowledge active in us. Otherwise we may be tempted to walk and behave as though the Scriptures are merely more words that have been written and recorded in time with the intention of helping us think a certain way about things. They are so much more! They are the very Life that bears witness to the character and expression of the One Who is all Authority! And in every place that "*it is written*" the Word has been given to make alive within us that very Truth that has been spoken from the mouth of the Father and accomplished in Jesus Christ His Son.

The One Who has created everything that is in existence will manifest the very thing we will believe Him for according to His Word. No matter what the enemy may bring against us or what need may arise, His Word continues to produce Life in all we ask according to His Will. This fertile harvest is produced by the germinating work of faith and belief in what He has already accom-

plished. He is our Savior and the Giver of every good and perfect gift His Salvation holds. And even as the grain of wheat falls from the original stock and creates many more new stocks of wheat, so the Word continues to create Life in every situation for the believer. Abundant Life! Eternal Life! From the First-Born Son, many sons are born; and from each new son more seeds of Life are sown.

Oh praise the Lord our God forever! Be encouraged today, dear ones. Jesus is Alive and His Word is Truth! In the shadows of death that surround us in this valley, remember always that the Light shines in our hearts and the Power of His Word is Living and Active within us! Amen!

Devotion Five

"PUT ON THE FULL ARMOR OF GOD"

"Finally, be strong in the Lord, and in the strength of His might. Put on the full armor of God, that you may be able to stand firm against the schemes of the devil. For our struggle is not against flesh and blood, but against the rulers, against the powers, against the world forces of this darkness, against the spiritual forces of wickedness in the heavenly places. Therefore, take up the full armor of God, that you may be able to resist in the evil day, and having done everything, to stand firm." **Ephesians 6:10-13**

Life and Light are provided to us by Divine instruction in this account of Holy Scripture. Heavenly insight is given as to where the struggles in our life originate and what we must know to stand firm against the evil schemes of the devil. We are enlightened by God's Word to the fact that our own strength is no match for the enemy.

However, Galatians 2:20 reminds those who are "*born again*" of the Spirit of God, that it is no longer we who live, but Christ now lives in us. He has become our Strength! Therefore, we must not give into the temptation of trying to perfect in the flesh what we began in the Spirit (Gal. 3:3). To do so will only set us up for failure. We must remember that it is in our "*weaknesses*" that His "*Strength*" is perfected and through Him we shall do valiantly.

We also learn that when called into battle, a soldier is given weapons and covering shields. He is taught the strategies of the enemy and how to watch for hidden snares. Paul is alerting us to the fact that our battle is not one of the flesh realm but rather one of the spiritual. He therefore instructs us that even as soldiers wear earthly armor in physical battles, we too must put on heavenly armor to withstand the spiritual battles.

This Divine equipment is not rationed to help us win, however, for the battle belongs to the Lord and the Victory has already been accomplished. It is instead given to protect us from the devices of the evil one who hopes to deceive us. It is his intention to keep us from walking out the wondrous and victorious life that has already been won for us in Jesus! We know by the Living Word that our Savior has completely disarmed the rulers and authorities that operate within the realm of darkness. He has forever triumphed over them (Col. 2:15)! We must be settled in this confidence daily in order to stand strong against Satan's schemes.

The word "*schemes*" in the Greek is *"methodeia."* It is the word from which we derive our English word "*methods*." It means *"trickery"* or *"to lie in wait." Webster's Dictionary* defines "*method*" in part as *"a discipline, a systematic plan, procedure, technique, or a process for obtaining an object."* In *Webster's* the word "*schemes*"

is defined as "*a plan or program of action, a systematic or organized framework.*"

So we see that there is a very systematic, intelligent, and orderly plan put forth in the "*schemes*" of the enemy. Trickery is woven into every fiber of his tactics as he lies in wait looking for opportunity. That is why we are instructed in Matthew 10:16 to "*be shrewd as serpents, and innocent as doves.*" We are to be a people of peace and yet "*cunning*" (*skillful and knowledgeable*) in our encounters with the enemy's strategies. We are to remain alert.

The Full Armor of God is given not only to protect us but also to make us aware of those places we can be vulnerable or left open to Satan's demonic tactics. It is imperative that we put on each piece daily with the confidence that this heavenly insulation will keep us safe and unharmed no matter what the enemy may be purposing to bring against us.

The Helmet of Salvation covers our mind to keep it sound because we know we have a Savior Who will give us understanding in all things. As His legitimate children who have been regenerated by His Spirit in "*new birth*" reality, we now have the "*Mind of Christ*" (1 Cor. 2:16). The Helmet of Salvation is also a protection against the lies of the enemy because the mind is where he always originates his greatest deceptions. 2 Corinthians 10:3-5 assures us: "*For though we walk in the flesh, we do not war according to the flesh, for the weapons of our warfare are not of the flesh, but divinely powerful for the destruction of fortresses. We are destroying speculations and every lofty thing raised up against the knowledge of God, and we are taking every thought captive to the obedience of Christ.*" Because of Salvation's assurance, we are empowered in Christ Jesus our Savior to set our minds in full and complete agreement with all His Word has promised us.

Our loins, which symbolize procreation or birth, are girded with Truth, again reminding us that we have been "*born again*" in Jesus Christ our Lord and are now "*new creations*" in Him. In 2 Corinthians 5:17, we are given this eternal confidence: "*Therefore if any man is in Christ, he is a new creature; the old things passed away; behold new things have come.*" No matter how much our past may try to haunt us with vain regrets and sorrows, God's Word declares that we are no longer that person. We have died with Christ. All the old things of our sinful natures have passed away and are buried in the sea of forgiveness. And because we have shared in His death, we now also share in His Glorious Resurrection! Jesus is our Savior and all Authority and the One Who will guard over the Salvation He has made sure in us. We may still stumble and fall but His Sacred Blood will continue to speak vindication on our behalf. By way of His gift of repentance and the Holy Spirit's continuing work of Sanctification, we are assured the guarantee that He is forever faithful to cleanse us of all unrighteousness. In "*new birth*" reality, Galatians 2:20 writes the epitaph upon the tombstone of our old nature: "*I have been crucified with Christ; and it is no longer I who live, but Christ lives in me; and the life which I now live in the flesh I live by faith in the Son of God who loved me, and delivered Himself up for me.*"

The Breastplate of Righteousness protects our hearts from being condemned by either the enemy or ourselves. By His Grace, we have been fully cleansed and vindicated in Christ Jesus our Lord. In 2 Corinthians 5:21, we are assured that: "*He made Him who knew no sin to be sin on our behalf, that we might become the righteousness of God in Him.*" We must never forget this forever Promise! The enemy loves to taunt us with the resume of our sinful past. He will whisper reminders that we

were idolaters, adulterers, fornicators and much more. But 1 Corinthians 6:11 will shut his mouth with perfect Atonement declaration: "*And such were some of you; but you were washed, but you were sanctified, but you were justified in the name of the Lord Jesus Christ, and in the Spirit of our God.*" May His Name be praised forever!

And in light of this Eternal Atonement security, our feet have been shod with the preparation of the Gospel of Peace. This Sacred covering protects us as we walk through the valley of the shadow of death to take the Good News of Salvation to those who are still dead in their trespasses. Because we now have peace with the Father through Christ Jesus our Lord, we can proclaim that same reconciliation oneness to those who yet remain separated from Him by sin's barrier. Isaiah 52:7 proclaims: "*How lovely on the mountains are the feet of him who brings good news, who announces peace and brings good news of happiness, who announces salvation, and says to Zion, 'Your God reigns!'*"

As ambassadors for Jesus, we have been commissioned in His Anointing Power to carry His Eternal Truth throughout all the earth. In both Isaiah 61:1-2 and Luke 4:18-20, this Holy mandate is recorded: "*The Spirit of the Lord is upon Me, because He anointed Me to preach the gospel to the poor. He has sent Me to proclaim release to the captives, and recovery of sight to the blind, to set free those who are downtrodden, to proclaim the favorable year of the Lord.*" Freely we have been given and freely we will give. And may we bring glory to His Name forever!

As we are serving Him on the front lines of the battle over men's souls, the Shield of Faith extinguishes all the flaming missiles of the evil one. These weapons are often fired from the launching pad of the tongue. James 3:6 describes the tongue in this way: "*And the tongue is a fire, the very world of iniquity; the tongue is set among our*

***members as that which defiles the entire body, and sets on fire the course our life, and is set on fire by hell.*"** **Through the words of men, Satan's lies and false accusations can bombard the believer's heart like torpedoes. Sometimes we even accuse ourselves as we unwittingly repeat what the enemy is whispering to us in our thoughts. But all praise to our God! Jesus is the Author and Perfecter of our faith (Heb. 12:2). He now stands as Vindicator between the false accuser and the brethren. And when the enemy "*prowls about as a roaring lion seeking someone to devour*" (1 Peter 5:8), the Shield of Faith will hold him at bay and stop him dead in his tracks. Our faith in the Promises of God, and the vindication of Jesus on our behalf, will enable us to resist him and "*as it is written*" he will flee away (James 4:7)! Remember, Jesus is our Righteousness, therefore, our worth is now found in Him.**

The Sword of the Spirit, which is the Word of God, is the weapon that is wielded against and utterly destroys all the evil one's purposes. By the Power of His Truth, every lie, deception and falsehood is annihilated. Revelation 19:11-16 gives heart-stirring description of the One Who Himself is the Living Word:

> ***"And I saw heaven opened; and behold, a white horse, and He who sat upon it is called Faithful and True; and in righteousness He judges and wages war. And His eyes are a flame of fire, and upon His head are many diadems; and He has a name written upon Him which no one knows except Himself. And He is clothed with a robe dipped in blood; and His name is called The Word of God. And the armies which are in heaven, clothed in fine linen, white and clean, were following Him on white horses. And from His mouth comes a sharp sword, so that with it He may smite the nations; and he will rule them***

with a rod of iron; and He treads the wine press of the fierce wrath of God, the Almighty. And on His robe and on His thigh He has a name written, 'KING OF KINGS, AND LORD OF LORDS!' "

There is no force in Hell or on earth that will ever be able to negate the Living Word of God! He reigns Eternally Supreme! His Truth has been forever settled in Heaven and the one who puts their trust in Him will never be ashamed nor will they be disappointed.

Oh beloved, let us continue to pray for and encourage one another to stand strong against our adversary by taking up and putting on the Full Armor of God each day. We are insulated in His Love and protected by His Grace. Nothing the enemy may attempt to do will be able to break through this Holy Spirit barrier.

Together we stand, and firm we remain, for the Lord our God is our Strength and our Salvation. Praise His Name forever!

Devotion Six

"THE HOLY SPIRIT IS OUR HELPER"

"Now the serpent was more crafty than any beast of the field which the Lord God had made. And he said to the woman, "Indeed, has God said, 'You shall not eat from any tree of the garden'?" And the woman said to the serpent, "From the fruit of the trees of the garden we may eat; but from the fruit of the tree which is in the middle of the garden, God has said, 'You shall not eat from it or touch it, lest you die.' " And the serpent said to the woman, "You surely shall not die! For God knows that in the day you eat from it your eyes will be opened, and you will be like God, knowing good and evil." When the woman saw that the tree was good for food, and that it was a delight to the eyes, and that the tree was desirable to make one wise, she took from its fruit and ate; and she gave also to her husband with her, and he ate. Then the eyes of both of them were opened, and they knew that they were naked; and they sewed fig leaves together and made themselves loin coverings." **Genesis 3:1-7**

"Indeed, has God said?" These four words, fueled with Hell's fire, sit at the very pinnacle of all unrighteousness, blasphemy and pride. They are the catalyst to every doubt and unbelief and are at the heart of every temptation that Satan originates. On the platform of this one statement, the father of lies built a weapon of deception that came crushing down on the beautiful paradise the Lord God had prepared and freely given to His children. It was the thief's intention from the beginning to rob, kill and destroy. (John 10:10)

With fierce intention and deadly zeal, the enemy continues in his schemes of death and destruction. However, we have not been left alone to fend for ourselves in this spiritual battle. The Holy Spirit is our Helper and has been given to lead us into all Truth (John 16:13). As we yield our hearts to Him, He will instruct us and protect us from falling prey to the enemy's devices in the evil day.

Through the Holy Spirit's inspiration, we are alerted to the pitfalls in which we can become vulnerable to the enemy's schemes. If we know how and where he will strike, we can then be prepared and girded up by the Power of God's Word to resist and stand firm. By way of this insight, Paul writes in 2 Corinthians 11:3: *"But I am afraid, lest as the serpent deceived Eve by his craftiness, your minds should be led astray from the simplicity and purity of devotion to Christ."* Paul is saying we must look back to the beginning to gain wisdom to know how this crafty serpent captivated Eve's mind. As we are given insight to how the enemy led her astray from complete dependence upon the One True God, and pure devotion to Him alone, we can safeguard ourselves against this same demonic tactic.

It is interesting that the Hebrew word for "*serpent*" finds its origin in the root word "*nachash*," which means

***"divine enchanter"* or *"to whisper."* An enchanter is a sorcerer. And to enchant means to influence by charms and incantations. It also means to bewitch or attract and move deeply. Satan's persuasions are always fueled with bewitching enticements. We must remember this fact so that we will not succumb to his methods. And we must take heed to the written Word of God for it holds within it all wisdom, insight and enlightenment in the true knowledge of Him. As we learn from those who have gone before us, and we continue to walk in the Light, our footing will remain sure and we will not stumble or fall.**

So as we look back with instructional wisdom, we learn that the Corinthians had been bothered by false apostles who were preaching another Jesus and another gospel. The same one that had tempted Eve in the garden was drawing them away from being single-minded and undefiled in their worship of the Lord. They were listening to man instead of the Holy Spirit.

Because Satan's realm is one of witchcraft his mode of operation always involves the twisting or distortion of God's Word. It is the adversary's intention to captivate man's mind and convince him to lean on his own understanding rather than to trust in the Lord with all his heart (Proverbs 3:5). The lure Satan casts is always enticing to the eyes and desirable to the flesh.

In the garden, not only did he tempt Eve to doubt what God had said, but in his shrewdness he planted the thought that the Creator of the universe was not completely loving, giving and just. The whispered suggestion was "*what good thing is God withholding from you Eve?*" And once he had her attention, the trap had been set; for now Eve's mind was engaged by him and her thoughts had been taken captive by his lies. In her effort to deal with the serpent from her own knowledge, she added a restriction that the Lord God had never imposed

upon her or Adam. God never said that they were not to touch the forbidden tree; only that they were not to eat from it (Genesis 2:17). Thus was birthed self-made religion which carries with it burdens and false decrees such as "*do not handle*" and "*do not touch*" (Col. 2:20-23). It is man's vain attempt, through his own futile efforts, to satisfy a perfect God by way of his self-imposed restrictions. Just like the fig leaves Adam and Eve sewed for themselves, man's religious ordinances cover him temporarily but in the end still leave him naked. Without being covered with the white robe of Jesus' Righteousness, mankind remains exposed by sin's shame.

In His paradise, the Father had provided his children with all that was beautiful and good. Anything He withheld was only that which would harm or destroy them. They were free of worry and the burden of fending for themselves. But once Eve moved out of the safety of her Creator's covering and complete reliance upon His Word, she had taken the first step to destruction. In fact, at the moment she gave attention to the enemy's voice the damage had already begun. Because Eve had set out alone without her Savior she had become vulnerable to Satan's schemes. And now without God's Holy counsel to guide and protect her, she was led to make judgments influenced by the lies the serpent told her. These deceptions were fed by what her eyes beheld, what her own understanding dictated to her, and by the lure of the lofty ambition to be like God. Satan had drawn her into the destructive web of his own prideful nature and consequently sin had its way in her. Eve then gave the forbidden fruit of disobedience to her husband and he ate as well. Sin loves company and is not satisfied until its poison has infected as many victims as possible.

Their eyes were now opened to the reality of their folly and the serpent's lie was exposed, but it was too late

to turn back. Just as God had spoken, Adam and Eve were now spiritually dead and eternally separated from their heavenly Father. Sin's destructive consequences had caused a chasm between them and their Creator. This great divide between life and death was so insurmountable that they would never be able to cross its barrier on their own. With the hindsight of vain regrets, Adam and Eve realized that before sin's net had been cast they had known only life and blessing and all that was good. Now in the snare of disobedience, their eyes were opened and they knew evil as well. Where they had once been blessed they were now cursed. The enemy would tenaciously continue to taunt them and the shadow of death would be their constant companion; for the wages of sin demanded a just penalty. Every man and woman born from their seed would now inherent their DNA of spiritual death. In this lost condition, true rest would forever escape them and their offspring as they would continue striving to redeem themselves and cover their own shame. Through the sin of arrogance and rejection of God's Word, man had elected himself as the judge between good and evil. No longer was he completely dependent on His Creator in obedience to His commandments and judgments, but was now a slave to sinful pride. From this point on, man would do what he deemed to be right in his own eyes (Proverbs 21:2).

But the God of Love made a way of escape even before the foundation of the world. He provided mankind with the help we so desperately needed and has granted us the way back to the Father. In His very great Love and Mercy, Jesus Christ, the Pure and Spotless Lamb of God, offered Himself up on the wooden beam of a cross and bridged the gap between the Father and man. *"He made Him who knew no sin to be sin on our behalf, that we might become the righteousness of God in Him."* (2 Cor. 5:21)

The pre-curse relationship between us and our Father has been reinstated through the shed Blood of the Messiah of God. The debt for the penalty of sin has been paid in full! To those who believe, this awesome Salvation has been granted, and we are now once again "*one*" with Him. Intimacy between us and our Father has been restored. Jesus is the Keeper of our souls, and in our "*new birth*" reality we live and move and have our being in complete dependence on Him. The Living Word is the Lamp that lights our path and leads us in the way we should go (Ps. 119:105). And the life which we now live in the flesh, we live by faith in the Son of God Who loved us and delivered Himself up for us. (Gal. 2:20)

It is good we are reminded of these things. For as we contemplate the magnificent Love of our God, we also remember that our adversary, the devil, continues to prowl about like a roaring lion seeking someone to devour (1 Peter 5:8). His tactics have not changed and neither has his nature. He was a murderer from the beginning and does not stand in the truth because there is no truth in him (John 8:44). The path he walks is lined with the stones of prideful unrighteousness and rejection of God's Word. And his rebellion forms the cloak of darkness which surrounds him. As Satan has from the beginning, he continues to tempt the unsuspecting by way of his schemes of deception. His hope is to lead to destruction as many as he can persuade to follow.

That is why the Father has provided us with a Helper who remains with us. He has given Him to lead us into all Truth and to establish us in His Eternal Kingdom purposes. In Him we have been called as a Chosen Race, a Royal Priesthood, a Holy Nation, a People for God's Own Possession. We are His ambassadors and as His voice in the earth we are anointed to proclaim the excel-

lencies of Him who has called us out of darkness into His marvelous Light. (1 Peter 2:9)

"So let us know, let us press on to know the Lord" **(Hosea 6:3). By the Power of His Truth, we shall not be deceived nor shall we be led astray. As we keep our eyes fixed on Jesus, the Holy Spirit will continue to remind us that we are forgiven, and we are loved! We shall not be conquered nor shall we be destroyed! The Lord of Hosts is our Champion and He has defeated Satan forever! In our Savior we shall be forever victorious! Praise His Name saints of the Most High God and give Him all Honor and Glory. Amen**

Devotion Seven

"SECURE IN HIM"

Though the fig tree should not
blossom,
And there be no fruit
on the vines,
Though the yield of the
olive should fail,
And the fields produce no
food,
Though the flock should be cut
off from the fold,
And there be no cattle in the
stalls,
Yet I will exult in the Lord,
I will rejoice in the God of
my salvation.
The Lord God is my strength,
And He has made my feet
like hinds' feet,
And makes me walk on my
high places.

Habakkuk 3:17-19

This beautiful expression of faith was intended to be sung with stringed accompaniment. It is a song of praise to the Lord God, Who is faithful to His Word no matter how our circumstances may attempt to convey otherwise. In spite of what the enemy is purposing, God's Word remains ever true and sure.

The name "*Habakkuk*" means "*Love's Embrace*." It gives us a picture of our Abba Father holding us close to His heart and shielding us with the Promise that He will carry us safely through every trial, valley or time of want. His Salvation provides all we will ever need, no matter what has come against us. When we have come to know our God and His faithfulness, we can then stand strong in His Strength. Though storms rage against us, we will not be shaken.

The Book of Habakkuk is an account of personal dialogue between the prophet (who was also a music minister in the Temple) and the Lord God. At the time of its writing, there was tyranny and oppression in the land at the hands of the Babylonians, and Judah's spiritual condition was at an all-time low (Hab. 1:2-4). Lawlessness was rampant, and hope on every front seemed bleak. In the midst of this great suffering, Habakkuk cried out to God for help and understanding. Even though he knew *"God's eyes are too pure to approve evil, and He cannot look on wickedness with favor,"* it seemed to this prophet that the Lord was remaining silent in the midst of such devastation. (Hab. 1:13)

In His answer to Habakkuk, Yahweh instructs His servant to record the vision of the things to come at the appointed time. God assures him that all He has declared by His Word will manifest in His perfect way and timetable. *"It hastens toward the goal, and it will not fail though it tarries, wait for it; for it will certainly come, it will not delay"* (Hab. 2:3). In the period of waiting, the righteous

are to live by faith (Hab. 2:4, Heb. 10:38). Our God is in control. His Word will not fail. We are completely safe in Him.

This knowledge caused Habakkuk to reverence the Lord and sing his song of praise. We, too, sing the song of praise to our Awesome God. No matter what is going on around us or how great our struggle, we will exult in the Lord. We will rejoice in the God of our Salvation for the Lord is our Strength! (Hab. 3:18)

The Hebrew word for "*strength*" in this passage is "*chayil,*" which means "*power, great might, an army, efficiency, wealth, and valiance.*" God is our provision and our supplier in every place of want or need. (Ps. 23:1)

God's Word makes our feet to be like "*hinds' feet*" and enables us to walk securely as we tread on high places. In the days of old, the "*high places*" were mountains and hills where idols were erected and worshipped. These "*high places*" still exist in the spiritual realm. Upon these pinnacles of darkness Satan has erected his falsehoods and deceptions by which he seeks to be worshipped.

But for those who have been "*born again*" and sealed by the Holy Spirit, the Father leads us to the "*Rock that is higher than I*" (Ps. 61:2). Knowing God's Truth sets us free from the snare of the enemy and empowers us to walk above our circumstances. His Light exposes every lie and falsehood the enemy brings against us and by the Power of His faithful Promises we trample down the idols of fear, unbelief, confusion and doubt.

Our feet have been shod with the preparation of the Gospel of Peace (Eph. 6:15); and we can now stand firm because He is faithful to all He has spoken. This assurance keeps us calm in times of turbulence. And as we stand on the Rock of His Word, we will not stumble for we will remain firmly planted upon His Truth. Because we can trust His Promises, we are kept in His Shalom.

In light of this confidence, we echo the words of David the psalmist: *"I waited patiently for the Lord; and He inclined to me, and heard my cry. He brought me up out of the pit of destruction, out of the miry clay; and He set my feet upon a rock making my footsteps firm. And He put a new song in my mouth, a song of praise to our God; many will see and fear, and will trust in the Lord."* (Ps. 40:1-3)

Continue to sing His praises, beloved. You are secure in Him!

Devotion Eight

"IF THE WORLD HATES YOU"

"Beloved, do not be surprised at the fiery ordeal among you, which comes upon you for your testing, as though some strange thing were happening to you; but to the degree that you share the sufferings of Christ, keep on rejoicing; so that also at the revelation of His glory, you may rejoice with exultation. If you are reviled for the name of Christ, you are blessed, because the Spirit of glory and of God rests upon you. By no means let any of you suffer as a murderer, or thief, or evildoer, or a troublesome meddler; but if anyone suffers as a Christian, let him not feel ashamed, but in that name let him glorify God. For it is time for judgment to begin with the household of God; and if it begins with us first, what will be the outcome for those who do not obey the gospel of God? AND IF IT IS WITH DIFFICULTY THAT THE RIGHTEOUS IS SAVED, WHAT WILL BECOME OF THE GODLESS MAN AND THE SINNER? Therefore, let those also who suffer according to the will of God entrust

their souls to a faithful Creator in doing what is right." **1 Peter 4:12-19 (Emphasis NASB)**

As followers of Christ Jesus, we will share in His sufferings. The Greek word for "*share*" in the 1 Peter 4:12-19 passage is *"koinoneo,"* which means *"to be a partaker with."* But it is associated with the word *"koinonos,"* which is translated "*companion.*"

There is nothing we can add to the sufferings Jesus bore for us on the Cross. His Sacrifice was complete and perfect. But when we walk with Him as His companions, we are then associated with Him. And as the world hated and still hates Him, we are also hated because we are now His and are no longer of the world. What they say about Him, they will say about us. True believers will be reviled. The Greek word for "*reviled*" is *"blasphemeo,"* from which our English word "*blaspheme*" is derived. It means "*to speak impiously about or to defame.*"

No matter how much the world rebels against or ridicules the Truth of God's Word it remains all Authority; for it has forever been settled in Heaven! It is Life to His children but foolishness to those who are perishing (1 Cor. 1:18). The more Jesus has His way in us and we are increasingly conformed into His image, the less the world will understand us and the more we will be reviled. But the Lord declares that we are to count it all joy! For when we are being confronted by the spirit of the world's darkness and ridiculed because of our love for Jesus, we are blessed because the Spirit of Glory and of God rests upon us, and He is glorified in our midst.

Because of the magnitude of this Holy calling in Him, 1 Peter 4:17 declares that judgment begins in the household of God. This refining fire comes for the testing of hearts and is the litmus test of the legitimacy of "*new birth.*" The Greek word for "*judgment*" is *"krima,"*

which means *"a decision for or against."* Jesus declares in Matthew 12:30: *"He who is not with Me is against Me; and he who does not gather with Me scatters."* Therefore, there is warning for those who do not obey the gospel of God. The Greek meaning here for *"do not obey"* (*"apeitheo"*) means to *"disbelieve willfully and perversely."*

Difficulties arise between those who believe the Word and those who do not. People who hold different citizenship can never realize genuine unity nor will they truly share anything of God in common. They may walk side by side and even gather together in church, but the realms in which they exist are in complete opposition. A true child of God holds citizenship in Heaven (Phil. 3:20), and is a child of the Light. Those who are yet of the world hold their citizenship in the realm of death and are children of the darkness.

Genuine faith in His Word is the deciding factor in Salvation's assurance. To believe the Word of God means more than just a mental assent for even the demons believe and shudder (James 2:19). True belief involves Covenant and oneness with God. It results in complete surrender and obedience to His Word. Because of this uncompromised devotion to the Lord, those who are truly His will suffer resistance from the world. However, Scripture gives clear distinction between the sufferings that are endured because of sin's consequences and the Sacred sufferings that are experienced by those who are identified with the work of His Cross. *"Therefore, let those who suffer according to the will of God entrust their souls to a faithful Creator in doing what is right"* (1 Peter 4:19). This is very pleasing in His sight.

Because life and death hang in the balance of Salvation's reality we must continue to speak His Truth in Love to those who are yet perishing. The Lord desires that none would be destroyed, but that all would believe

and be reconciled to Him. Only in knowing the One Who alone is Truth is man set free from the bondage of sin and death. Lies can offer false comfort, but they will never provide freedom or give Eternal Life!

As we continue in this Great Commission, it pleases the Father when He sees our unwavering faith in Him in the midst of the enemy's onslaughts. Our labor of love in reaching out to the lost in His Name touches His heart deeply. And as we worship Him in Spirit and in Truth, our praises and heart-felt devotion to Him fill His Temple as a sweet fragrance before His Throne of Grace. These things are of great virtue to the Living God.

Salvation is free, but discipleship comes at a cost. Remember the words of Jesus in John 15:18-21: ***"If the world hates you, you know that it has hated Me before it hated you. If you were of the world, the world would love its own; but because I chose you out of the world, therefore the world hates you. Remember the word that I said to you, 'A slave is not greater than his master.' If they persecuted Me, they will also persecute you; if they kept My word, they will keep yours also. But all these things they will do to you for My name's sake, because they do not know the One who sent Me."***

As we continue to follow in His footsteps, let us not grow weary of doing what is right; and may we continue to love the lost even as the Father first loved us when we were yet dead in our trespasses. We must continue to shine the Light of Jesus into the darkness of the world to lead them back into the safety of His Love. We must tell them the Truth whether they listen or not. And whatever sufferings we may endure in this heart-felt endeavor will be as nothing in light of His glories that await us. His "*well done good and faithful servant*" will be all that matters as we behold His good pleasure and bow down in forever worship of Him!

All Praise and Glory belongs forever to the One Who is our Salvation!

Devotion Nine

"JESUS OUR REST & SAFETY"

"Gracious is the Lord, and righteous; yes, our God is compassionate. The Lord preserves the simple; I was brought low, and He saved me. Return to your rest, O my soul, for the Lord has dealt bountifully with you. For Thou has rescued my soul from death, my eyes from tears, my feet from stumbling. I shall walk before the Lord in the land of the living." **Psalm 116:5-9**

Beloved, our God is an Awesome God! How excellent and marvelous is His Word!

When our soul is in turmoil, there is a place of rest to which we can return. The Word will take us there as we are reminded of that exact moment the Holy Spirit came and rescued us. It is here that we were set free from the chains of sin and death that held us captive. At the very instant Salvation was manifested to us, we were transferred from the *"land of the dead"* (Eph. 2:1) to the *"land of the living"* (Luke 20:38). Our physical feet still touch the terra firma of this planet, but our citizenship is now

in Heaven where we live, move and have our being in Christ Jesus our Lord. (Phil. 3:20)

We can lose sight of this truth, however, as we walk through this valley where the shadow of death surrounds us (Ps. 23:4, Is. 9:2, Matt. 4:16). If we are not being washed by the Living Water regularly, we can pick up the stench of the world's death and begin walking as though it still holds power over us. We need to be reminded every day that because we abide in His Word and His Word abides in us, we now know the Truth and the Truth has set us free! In His Compassion and Mercy the Father has dealt so bountifully with us. We deserved death but by the Precious Blood of Jesus we have been released from the penalty of sin's consequences. He ransomed us from eternal damnation and set our feet on the solid ground of His Word. Death has been forever defeated by His Glorious Resurrection!

Ephesians 2:4-10 assures us that: ***"God being rich in mercy, because of His great love with which He loved us, even when we were dead in our transgressions, made us alive together with Christ (by grace you have been saved), and raised us up with Him, and seated us with Him in the heavenly places in Christ Jesus, in order that in the ages to come He might show the surpassing riches of His grace in kindness toward us in Christ Jesus. For by grace you have been saved through faith; and that not of yourselves, it is the gift of God; not as a result of works, that no one should boast. For we are His workmanship created for good works, which God prepared beforehand, that we should walk in them."***

Only in the land of Life, through His finished work, can we ever hope to walk in a manner worthy of the mandate by which we have been called (Eph. 4:1). In Jesus alone do we find true rest because He has already done all that is needed to fulfill the Holy demands of God's perfection.

As we live, move and have our being in Him, the works He has already prepared beforehand supernaturally flow through us. Therefore, as we decrease and He increases, His fruits of Righteousness and Holiness will manifest in abundant measure.

And as this Sanctifying work of Sacred humility continues in us, Psalm 116:6 declares that: "*The Lord preserves the simple.*" Are you simple, dear one? If you are, rejoice and be glad; for the Lord delights in such as these. The Greek meaning for "*simple*" (*pethi*) is "*open-minded.*" In *Webster's Dictionary* one of the definitions for "*open*" is "*willing to hear and accept.*"

As the Holy Spirit grants us spiritual ears to hear, may we be made even more willing, in yielded heart surrender, to believe and accept all His magnificent Word has promised. It is my prayer that the "*Mind of Christ*" would manifest continuously in us, so that double-mindedness would no longer be an option. How thankful I am for our Advocate for when we are faithless, He remains Faithful! (2 Tim. 2:13)

Let our hearts be glad today and every day that we remain on this planet longing for His Return. Rest in His Love beloved; you are safe in Him. And always remember that as God's children, every place we tread becomes "Holy Ground" because of Jesus within us. We are no longer to walk as though we are still dead. He has made us alive together with Him. In Dunamis Resurrection Power, we have been rescued from death forever!

Time is short. The harvest is still great. Proclaim His Word wherever He leads you. And remember - be thankful! For He has done great and marvelous things, and He is so Good! Amen!

Devotion Ten

"CHOOSE YOU THIS DAY"

"And Elijah came near to all the people and said, 'How long will you hesitate between two opinions? If the Lord is God, follow Him; but if Baal, follow him.'" 1 Kings 18:21

This challenge made by Elijah on Mt. Carmel came to 450 prophets of Baal, and also to the Israelites, who had forsaken the commandments of the Lord and were putting their hope in this false god. The name "*Baal*" means "*lord or master.*" The plural word, "*Baalim,*" was used for the different manifestations of this false deity and was also used to indicate that each local Baal had independent existence. Incense and sacrifice - even human sacrifice - were offered to the Baalim with the hope that their women, land and animals would become fertile.

When the Lord's people came into Canaan, they began to see Baal and Yahweh as the same deity. By adopting the belief system of the Canaanites and participating in their pagan customs, the Israelites compromised their knowledge of the One True God in exchange for fallen

man's foolish notions. They had meshed the counterfeit with the Truth.

Through His servant, Jehovah drew a clear line of distinction between Truth and falsehood. After Elijah's challenge to the people in 1 Kings 18:21, we learn that he built an altar to the Lord (1 Kings 18:31-35). We pick up in verses 36-37: "*Then it came about at the time of the offering of the evening sacrifice, that Elijah the prophet came near and said, "O Lord, the God of Abraham, Isaac and Israel, today let it be known that Thou art God in Israel, and that I am Thy servant, and that I have done all these things at Thy word. Answer me, O Lord, answer me, that this people may know that Thou, O Lord, art God, and that Thou hast turned their heart back again.*" Verse 38 records the Lord's answer: "*Then the fire of the Lord fell, and consumed the burnt offering and the wood and the stones and the dust, and licked up the water that was in the trench.*"

This mighty miracle manifested the reality and majesty of the One True God. He alone is Lord and there is no other! He will not share His Glory; His Holiness forbids it. God's Sanctifying Fire not only burned up the altar and everything that comprised it but also all the vain imaginations and opinions of man. For when the people saw it, they fell on their faces; and they said, "*The Lord, He is God; the Lord, He is God.*" (1 Kings 18:39)

Our God is a consuming Fire (Deut. 4:24 Heb. 12:29)! And this Holy Fire will continue its work until the day of the Lord when "*the heavens will pass away with a roar and the elements will be destroyed with intense heat, and the earth and its works will be burned up*" (2 Pet. 3:10). Only His Truth will remain. Only those who have been insulated by His Truth shall endure to the end and be Saved. (Matt. 24:13)

We must remember that though these things seem hard, it is for our welfare that we must hear them. They are given to protect us, for Love is the motivation behind every act of God. It is the all in all of His discipline and at the very core of His commands. It is what took Him to the Cross for us.

Psalm 19 provides a beautiful declaration of the testimonies and judgments of the Lord and why we should give heed to them. In verses 10 and 11, we are taught that *"they are more desirable than gold, yes, than much fine gold; sweeter also than honey and the drippings of the honeycomb. Moreover, by them Thy servant is warned; in keeping them there is great reward."* His Word warns us of danger and exposes those places the enemy has laid his net of destruction. The Lord's discipline calls us back to our Abba Father Who loves us and desires that we would reap the fullness of His Salvation.

Elijah's prayer in 1 Kings 18:36 bears this out when he cried: *"O Lord, the God of Abraham, Isaac and Israel, today let it be known that Thou art God in Israel, and that I am Thy servant, and that I have done all these things at Thy word. Answer me, O Lord, answer me, that this people may know that Thou, O Lord, art God, and that Thou hast turned their heart back again."* This prayer echoed the cry of God's heart. "Know Me and live! Return to Me and be washed and forgiven! Follow My Commandments and be blessed!" For it brings the Lord no pleasure to see the wicked perish (Ezek. 18:23), and He desires that all would be Saved. (1 Tim. 2:4)

In closing, let us consider that while the Holy Spirit is about His work of Salvation, there is an enemy who prowls about seeking to deceive and destroy. Satan is the master sculptor of every idol. The Baalim represent anything or anyone that would attempt to take the place

of, or join itself to, the One True Living God in our devotion, worship, love, or dependence upon.

In 2 Kings 17:41, a picture is given of how God's children can be ensnared by this evil persuasion: ***"So while these nations feared the Lord, they also served their idols; their children likewise and their grandchildren as their fathers did, so they do to this day."*** **While they were reverencing the Lord, they were also serving the Baalim of this world.**

Oh beloved, may the Holy Spirit help us to recognize the spirits of abomination that have crept into our midst in the Church. With His help, we must guard ourselves from these idols (1 John 5:21). We are called to worship the Lord in Spirit and in Truth (John 4:24) and to surrender our devotion to Him alone. Let us not be a people who, while reverencing the Lord, are looking at the same time to the counterfeits. The traditions, customs, psychology and philosophies of the world will not save us nor can they offer any real help or hope. Jesus is our Savior! Let us take comfort in knowing that He has provided all we will ever need by His Word. When we hear His Voice may we not harden our hearts to His discipline and warnings.

> ***"For whatever was written in earlier times was written for our instruction, that through perseverance and the encouragement of the Scriptures we might have hope. Now may the God Who gives perseverance and encouragement grant you to be of the same mind with one another according to Christ Jesus; that with one accord you may with one voice glorify the God and Father of our Lord Jesus Christ."*** **(Rom. 15:4-6)**

Hallelujah and Amen.

Devotion Eleven

"CONTENDERS FOR HIS TRUTH"

"Children, it is the last hour; and just as you heard that antichrist is coming, even now many anti-christs have arisen; from this we know that it is the last hour. They went out from us, but they were not really of us; for if they had been of us, they would have remained with us; but they went out, in order that it might be shown that they all are not of us. But you have an anointing from the Holy One, and you all know. I have not written to you because you do not know the truth, but because you do know it, and because no lie is of the truth. Who is the liar but the one who denies that Jesus is the Christ? This is the antichrist, the one who denies the Father and the Son. Whoever denies the Son does not have the Father; the one who confesses the Son has the Father also. As for you, let that abide in you which you heard from the beginning. If what you heard from the beginning abides in you, you also will abide in the Son and in the Father." **1 John 2:18-24**

We must come to the understanding that there is a spirit on this planet that is operating in complete hostility and opposition to the One True God. It is an intelligent spirit that carries with it a militant agenda to sit in the place of the Great I AM (Is. 14:13-14). This is the spirit of antichrist which has been birthed from Satan himself.

The word "*antichrist*" in the Greek is "*antichristos*" and means "*an opponent of the Messiah.*" It is a copulation of the words "*anti,*" which means "*against, instead of, or substitution for*" and "*Christos*" the "*anointed one.*"

As we glean from the Scripture verses of 1 John 2:18-24 we are given wisdom in recognizing this vessel of darkness. In verse 22, we read: *"Who is the liar but the one who denies that Jesus is the Christ? This is the antichrist, the one who denies the Father and the Son."* The Greek word for "*denies*" in this passage is "*arneomai.*" It gives the understanding that the liar is not only the one who *"rejects"* the reality that Jesus is the Christ, but also the one who "*contradicts"* this forever Truth. Verse 23 continues to warn that "*whoever denies* (or "*contradicts"*) *the Son does not have the Father; the one who confesses the Son has the Father also."* Man may say he believes in Jesus, but by adding to or taking away from His complete and perfect Sacrifice, their denials are blasphemous contradictions to the Truth.

The word "*confesses*" in this passage is the Greek word "*homologeo,*" which means "*of one mind,*" and "*to speak the same.*" Therefore, to truly confess Jesus as Lord is to be of one mind with Him and to speak only His unadulterated Word of Truth. 1 Corinthians 2:16 instructs us that true believers have been given the "*Mind of Christ.*" Therefore, what we speak of Him will be in complete agreement with what His Word has declared of Him.

The Holy Spirit has been given to lead us into all Truth (John 16:13). That is why in the 1 John 2 passage and in verse 27 we read: *"And as for you, the anointing which you received from Him abides in you, and you have no need for anyone to teach you; but as His anointing teaches you about all things, and is true and is not a lie, and just as it has taught you, you abide in Him."*

He is the Teacher, not man. He is the One Who shows the Way and reveals every lie that contradicts the Truth. He is the very Essence of the Word, which is all Truth, and He bears witness to that Truth in the spirit of a "*born again*" believer. This "*new man*" abides in the heavenly reality that has been made alive in him. As a legitimate child of God, he lives out his life in humbled surrender and reverential dependence upon the Lord Jesus his Savior. As a "*new creation*" he has now become one with Jesus Who is the Way, the Truth and the Life. The ones who "*went out*" (1 John 2:19), were never true believers. They had not been filled with the Holy Spirit; they had not been regenerated. Judas was one of these.

A person can say they know Jesus, but unless they have truly encountered the Great I AM, in heart circumcised repentance, they have only "*head knowledge*" of Him. If man has not been transferred from death unto Life through the Blood of Jesus and is now indwelt by the Holy Spirit, he has not become a "*new creature*" where the old things have passed away and new things have come (2 Cor. 5:17). In this unsaved condition, arrogance thrives and abominations and lies of every kind sit on the throne of pride. Here man operates and lives out his life dependant upon a wisdom that has been birthed from Hell, and which keeps him separated from the One Who gave His Own Life to Save him. This is the spirit of antichrist, and it is the seed from which every false religion known to man has originated.

But we, as the legitimate "*born again*" children of God, are encouraged with these Life-giving words: *"As for you, let that abide in you which you heard from the beginning. If what you heard from the beginning abides in you, you also will abide in the Son and in the Father*" (1 John 2:24). As we abide in His Truth, His Truth abides in us. And as we keep our eyes fixed on Jesus, the Living Word, we shall not be deceived or led astray.

Oh beloved ones, may we continue to be contenders for "*the faith that was once for all delivered to the saints*" (Jude 1:3). Every lie and falsehood will be brought into the Light and exposed. Only His Word will remain for it has been forever settled in Heaven.

And as we stand firmly on the Rock of our Salvation, Revelation 12:11 will be our triumphant cry: "*And they overcame him* (the accuser of the brethren vs. 10) *because of the blood of the Lamb and because of the word of their testimony, and they did not love their life even to death."*

Our God reigns, and He is coming for us soon! Worship Him and praise His Name forever!

Devotion Twelve

"THE POWER OF PRAYER"

"Elijah was a man with a nature like ours, and he prayed earnestly that it might not rain; and it did not rain on the earth for three years and six months. And he prayed again, and the sky poured rain, and the earth produced its fruit." **James 5:17**

We must go back to the account in 1 Kings 17, to more fully understand what James is conveying to us about Elijah and the power of a believer's prayer. Ahab became king over Israel in the 38th year of Asa, king of Judah, and he reigned 22 years. He erected an altar for Baal in the house of Baal, which he built in Samaria. It is recorded in Scripture that Ahab did more to provoke the Lord God than did all the kings of Israel who were before him. (1 Kings 16:33)

Baal worship was threatening the very existence of true worship of God in Israel. Elijah was raised up by the Holy Spirit at this critical time in history to call a drought upon this nation. By the Word of God, it would be given as a sign to Ahab and the Israelites that Jehovah

was the One True God. The Lord's intention was to bring them to repentance.

In the midst of this Divine drought, the Lord sent Elijah to a widow who lived in Zarephath. She had only a handful of flour and a little oil and was preparing with her son to die. Elijah told her not to fear and then prophesied: *"For thus says the Lord God of Israel, 'The bowl of flour shall not be exhausted, nor shall the jar of oil be empty, until the day that the Lord sends rain on the face of the earth'"* (1 Kings 17:13-14). Then in verses 15-16 we read: *"So she went and did according to the word of Elijah, and she and he and her household ate for many days. The bowl of flour was not exhausted nor did the jar of oil become empty, according to the word of the Lord which He spoke through Elijah."* How exciting to realize that in the time of lack, Jehovah-Jireh had provided unending supply!

But even in the midst of God's faithfulness we learn that the enemy was still on the prowl. After these things took place, the woman's son became sick and died. And yet no matter how bad things seem to be, God's miracle working power is only a prayer away for His children. Elijah called out to the Lord and stretched himself upon the child three times, asking that the child's life be restored. *"And the Lord heard the voice of Elijah, and the life of the child returned to him and he revived."* (1 Kings 17:17-22)

In this we see a prophetic foretelling. As Elijah stretched himself upon the child three times and sought the Lord on his behalf, another One would stretch Himself upon a cross to be offered up on mankind's behalf. At the precise and appointed time that the Father had determined before the foundation of the world, Jesus the Christ, God's Spotless and Precious Lamb, would satisfy sin's penalty in forever Sacred Atonement. Mankind had

died to sin, but after three days our beloved Savior would rise again in Glorious Resurrection Power that we might be forgiven and made alive forever with Him!

Therefore, we see that Elijah was a "type" of the One Who was to come as Savior of the world. The name "*Elijah*" means *"Jehovah is my God."* And now we are told in James that Elijah was a man with a nature like ours. But let us be clear about what that nature is; for Scripture is not referring to our flesh nature.

In 2 Peter 1:2-4 it is written: *"Grace and peace be multiplied to you in the knowledge of God and of Jesus our Lord; seeing that His divine power has granted to us everything pertaining to life and godliness, through the true knowledge of Him who called us by His own glory and excellence. For by these He has granted to us His precious and magnificent promises, in order that by them you might become partakers of the Divine nature, having escaped the corruption that is in the world by lust."* (Emphasis mine)

As partakers of His *"Divine Nature"* in *"new birth"* reality, we are called to be His vessels of Light and Truth to a dark and dying world. We are His ambassadors sent to herald Salvation's message and to show the way of escape to those who are still ensnared by Satan's corruption. God's arm of Grace reaches out to ransom those who are yet captivated in their carnal appetites and dead in their trespasses. As living testimonies, we proclaim the freedom from sin's slavery that has been granted to us in Jesus Christ our Lord. And it is in the forum of "*prayer*" where the angelic armies that aid us in this effort are dispatched to bring down the strongholds of the enemy and to thwart Satan's plans of destruction.

We are also called to "*pray*" for one another in the household of God especially when a brother has gone astray. This is what James is referring to in chapter 5 of our opening Scripture because in verses 19 and 20,

he goes on to say: *"My brethren, if any among you strays from the truth, and one turns him back, let him know that he who turns a sinner from the error of his way will save his soul from death, and will cover a multitude of sins."*

When we "*pray*" in the "*Name of Jesus,*" we are "*praying*" with His Authority. In verse 16 of the James Chapter 5 passage it is written: *"The effective prayer of a righteous man can accomplish much."* Clearly this Scripture is not referring to any righteousness of our own. In "*new birth*" reality, we have been made the righteousness of God in Christ Jesus the Lord (2 Cor. 5:21). It is only in light of His Holiness and Perfection that we can enter confidently into the Throne of God's Grace and make our requests known. In John 14:13-14, Jesus said: "*And whatever you ask in My name, that will I do, that the Father may be glorified in the Son. If you ask Me anything in My name, I will do it.*"

Further insight is also given as to how we are to "*pray,*" for we are told that Elijah *"prayed earnestly."* Both words in the Greek mean *"to worship."* Worship positions us within the Living Word's Presence where we are then given audience to ask of Him those things which are in accordance with His Promises. As we delight in Him, all we want is Him, and in Him is all we will ever need.

May our hearts be encouraged as His Word reminds us again that we truly are now "*new creations*" in Jesus. We have been delivered from our old sin nature and transferred into the Divine Nature of the One Who is now our Life. We are no longer slaves to the things of darkness, so let us set our minds to agree with what God has settled by His Word. In His forever Salvation confidence we are equipped to march on as the army He has called us to be.

As Elijah's prayer called forth the rain which produced fruit in the earth, so will the prayers that we

speak in the "*Name of Jesus*" call forth the Living Water of His Word which produces the fruits of Salvation in the soil of believing hearts. Therefore, let us continue to pray without ceasing for there is Resurrection Power in our prayers!

Be encouraged dear ones, for our God is Good, His Word is Truth, and He is coming again soon. Hallelujah!

Devotion Thirteen

"HUMBLE YOURSELF"

"Humble yourselves, therefore, under the mighty hand of God that He may exalt you at the proper time, casting all your anxiety upon Him, because He cares for you. Be of sober spirit, be on the alert. Your adversary, the devil, prowls about like a roaring lion, seeking someone to devour. But resist him, firm in your faith, knowing that the same experiences of suffering are being accomplished by your brethren who are in the world. And after you have suffered for a little while, the God of all grace, who called you to His eternal glory in Christ, will Himself perfect, confirm, strengthen and establish you. To Him be dominion forever and ever. Amen." **1 Peter 5:6-ll**

The word "*humble*" used in this passage is derived from the Greek word "*tapeinoo,*" which means *"to make low."* It is taken from the primary Greek word *"tapeinos,"* which is translated "*low-lying.*" We are called to submit ourselves unto God, which places us under His loving and protective Hand. Knowing He cares for us,

and that He is keeping us covered with His perfect Love, will cast all anxiety and fear away no matter what may be coming against us.

Scripture instructs us that while God turns His heart to the humble, He is fiercely opposed to the proud (1 Pet. 5:5). The word for "*proud*" in the Greek is "*hupereph-anos*," which means *"showing oneself above others."* The one who is proud arrogantly walks outside the covering of God and, therefore, exposes himself to the adversary. In this unprotected position he becomes an open target for the devil who prowls about like a roaring lion seeking someone to devour (vs. 8). But the humbled one is hidden under the Hand of God, where he is kept, protected and strengthened. In this submitted position, Divine Strength is being appropriated as the child of God is being readied to stand victoriously against the wiles of the devil. "*Thou hast also given me the shield of Thy Salvation, and Thy right hand upholds me*" (Ps. 18:35). Then at the proper time the Lord raises him up, for he is now equipped in his Savior to resist the enemy.

In our resisting, we do not remain hidden nor do we retreat. The Greek word for "*resist*" used in the 1 Peter 5:6-11 passage is "*anthistemi,"* which means "*to set against or withstand.*" It is the same word used in James 4:7 where he exhorts us to "*Submit therefore to God. Resist the devil and he will flee from you.*" We withstand and overcome the enemy by the power of the Blood of the Lamb, and the testimony that Jesus is now our Salvation! (Rev. 12:10-11)

"*What then shall we say to these things? If God is for us, who can be against us*?" (Rom. 8:31). By faith in the Lord, and the confidence that He is all Power and Authority, we will remain standing strong. His faithfulness to His Word is the solid ground upon which we stand. And as we trust in Him we shall not be ashamed or disappointed.

As to the sufferings shared in this present time of resisting the enemy we, with Paul, consider that they are "*not worthy to be compared with the glory that is to be revealed in us*" (Rom. 8:18). For after we have "*suffered*" for a little while, the God of all Grace, Who called us to His Eternal Glory in Christ, promises that He Himself will *perfect*, *confirm*, *strengthen* and *establish* us (1 Pet. 5:10). As we glean from the definitions of these words in the original language, we will come to a deeper understanding of the Holy Spirit's empowering provision that is held in this Promise.

The Greek word for "*suffered*" is "*pascho.*" It gives the understanding of *"feeling passion."* The Greek word for "*perfect*" is "*katartizo*" and means: *"to complete thoroughly."* The Greek word for "*confirm*" is "*sterizo*" and means: *"to turn resolutely in a certain direction and set fast."* The Greek word for "*strengthen*" is "*sthenoo*" and means: *"to confirm in spiritual knowledge and power."* And, finally, to "*establish*" which in Greek is *"themelioo"* means: *"to lay the foundation."*

His Truth is the foundation upon which we stand, therefore, we will not be shaken! He makes all things known to us by His Word as the Holy Spirit leads us into all Truth. And He has promised to bring to completion the good work He has begun in us (Phil. 1:6). Because of His faithfulness, we are strengthened in the assurance that He will do what He said He would. And in light of the integrity of His character we trust that *"God causes all things to work together for good to those who love God, to those who are called according to His purposes*" (Rom. 8:28). Therefore, no matter what is going on in our lives our God is in control and working out His highest and best for us.

Oh, what an Awesome God He is and how marvelous are His works! Praise Him always, and be strong in His

Strength, ransomed ones. And to Him, be all Dominion forever and ever. Amen!

Devotion Fourteen

"HIS GRACE IS SUFFICIENT"

"And because of the surpassing greatness of the revelations, for this reason, to keep me from exalting myself, there was given me a thorn in the flesh, a messenger of Satan to buffet me—to keep me from exalting myself! Concerning this I entreated the Lord three times that it might depart from me. And He has said to me, 'My grace is sufficient for you, for power is perfected in weakness.' Most gladly, therefore, I will rather boast about my weaknesses, that the power of Christ may dwell in me. Therefore I am well content with weaknesses, with insults, with distresses, with persecutions, with difficulties, for Christ's sake; for when I am weak, then I am strong." 2 Corinthians 12:7-10

While Paul was traveling into Macedonia on his third missionary journey, he encountered Titus and learned that his first letter to the Corinthians had accomplished much good. It had been severe because of serious sin issues but had produced a sincere repentance. However, there were still some in Corinth, who

denied that Paul was a true apostle of Jesus and were creating dissent among the brethren. Therefore much of 2 Corinthians is written in defense of his valid calling as a servant of God. He saw the converts in Corinth as his spiritual children and desired that they walk in Truth and Love.

In his attempts to convince them, Paul relates an experience about a man who was "*caught up*" to the third heaven (2 Cor. 12:2). Although he humbly points this amazing experience away from himself, it is clear from the whole context of Scripture that he is the man to whom he refers. As a side note, it is exciting to realize the phrase "*caught up*" (vs. 2, 4), is actually the Greek verb "*harpazo*" from which the meaning *"rapture"* is derived. It is the same word used in 1 Thessalonians 4:17 where Paul speaks about believers who are going to be "*caught up*" together in the clouds to meet the Lord in the air and be forever with Him. As a living witness, this beloved apostle experienced what will happen at the Rapture!

While in Paradise, Paul was given "*revelations*" that were of surpassing greatness. The word "*revelations,*" which in Greek is "*apokalupsis,*" means *"an uncovering."* It is derived from "*apokalupto*" meaning "*to uncover*" or *"reveal."* This word is used in Luke 10:21 where Jesus proclaims: *"I praise Thee, O Father, Lord of heaven and earth, that Thou didst hide these things from the wise and intelligent and didst reveal them to babes. Yes, Father for thus it was well-pleasing in Thy sight.*"

We are told that because of these revelations, in order to keep Paul from exalting himself or as the Greek translates "*boasting,*" he was given a thorn in the flesh which came as a messenger of Satan. The word "*messenger*" is the Greek word "*aggelos,"* which means *"one who brings tidings."* Things were being said to and about Paul that were a constant, deeply penetrating, pricking and

jabbing. This thorn served as reminder of the inadequacies of his human nature with its frailties and disappointments. Each word came as a strike of the fist as the Greek word for "*buffet*" conveys. Although he entreated the Lord three times that it would depart from him, something so much more wonderful was provided through another "*revelation*" to Paul. In answer to his plea, the Lord God proclaimed: "*My Grace is sufficient for you, for power is perfected in weakness." (Emphasis mine)*

The Grace of God! The unmerited favor of the King of kings and Lord of lords! Divine influence upon the heart which bears the beautiful reflection of the One Who is now the Life within a believer! The Living Word was revealing the Divine exchange realized in the "*born again*" child of God who by faith in Jesus is now equipped with all he will ever need in the Great I AM.

The message was: "Paul, your flesh and its weaknesses will not negate the Victory I have already accomplished for you. Neither your ability nor inability can hinder My Word from producing the works that will stand the test of fire. It is My Grace that manifests My Power in your life. When you come to the realization that apart from Me you can do nothing, but that all things are possible for God, it is then that you will serve Me in the confidence of My Power and Authority." (John 15:5, Matt. 19:26, Mark 10:27, Luke 18:27)

And that same Grace is forever sufficient for us as well beloved. The word "*sufficient*" is the Greek word *"arkeo,"* which means *"enough."* It is akin to the Greek word *"arego,"* which means *"to help, aid, and assist."* The Holy Spirit Who is our Helper moves and manifests His being most powerfully in us when we will acknowledge our weaknesses, and in holy surrender lean on the One Who alone is our Strength. It is just over the border of "self's end," that contentment is reached. In this place of

God centeredness, man's approval (whether our own or that of others) no longer holds authority over us. And our victory is no longer determined by our own strengths or weaknesses. In this Holy Spirit haven, the overcoming has already been realized, and therefore we are at peace.

Dear one, if you are a Blood-bought child of God, the Holy Spirit surely reveals Himself to you by His Word. So realize that, because the enemy opposes a saint who is empowered by the knowledge of God, the attacks will come. Nevertheless, there is rest and contentment for you today as you are strengthened in the revelation of Who He is within you. He is our Victory in every situation. Therefore, *"let the weak say I am strong!"* (Joel 3:10, 2 Cor. 12:10)

What joy and peace is found in the discovery that: *"I have been crucified with Christ; and it is no longer I who live, but Christ lives in me; and the life which I now live in the flesh I live by faith in the Son of God, who loved me, and delivered Himself up for me."* (Gal. 2:20)

Jesus! Elohim! The Supreme and Mighty God! Believe in Him, be confident and rejoice, and give all the Glory to Him forever! Amen.

Devotion Fifteen

"THE RENEWED MIND"

"If then you have been raised up with Christ, keep seeking the things above, where Christ is, seated at the right hand of God. Set your mind on the things above, not on the things that are on earth. For you have died and your life is hidden with Christ in God." **Colossians 3:1-3**

The Greek word for the phrase *"set your mind"* in this passage is "*phroneo*," which means *"to have understanding, to think."* What a man does or does not understand in his mind directly affects his behavior; *"for as a man thinks within himself, so he is"* (Proverbs 23:7). To set our mind implies in the Greek more than only thinking. It indicates exercising the mind toward our affections, will and moral considerations.

Ephesians 4:17-25 grants us holy insight into this premise: *"This I say therefore, and affirm together with the Lord, that you walk no longer just as the Gentiles also walk, in the futility of their mind, being darkened in their understanding, excluded from the life of God, because of the ignorance that is in them, because of the hardness of*

their heart; and they having become callous, have given themselves over to sensuality, for the practice of every kind of impurity with greediness. But you did not learn Christ in this way, if indeed you have heard Him and have been taught in Him, just as truth is in Jesus, that, in reference to your former manner of life, you lay aside the old self, which is being corrupted in accordance with the lusts of deceit, and that you be renewed in the spirit of your mind and put on the new self, which in the likeness of God has been created in righteousness and holiness of the truth. Therefore, laying aside falsehood, speak truth each one of you with his neighbor, for we are members of one another."

As we read those powerful words of exhortation, we realize that now more than ever, we are being called back to the faith that was once for all delivered to the saints (Jude 1:3); for there is much falsehood in our midst today. By the working of the enemy who vies for our minds, many doctrines of the world have crept into the Church with enticing persuasion. These hellish heresies are in complete opposition to the Truth and produce a fleshly people, who believe they are rich, and having become wealthy have need of nothing. They do not know that they are wretched, miserable, poor, blind and naked (Rev. 3:17). They operate in a wisdom that James tells us is not that which comes down from above, but is earthly, natural and demonic. (James 3:15)

But our merciful and loving Father provides the remedy by the gift of "*repentance,*" which literally means "*to change one's mind.*" Acts 3:19 exhorts us to: *"Repent therefore and return, that your sins may be wiped away, in order that times of refreshing may come from the presence of the Lord."*

We are beckoned by the Lord to turn away from every futile counterfeit of help or hope that false prophets have

set before us, and return to the Keeper of our soul (Ps. 121:7). As we look to Him, the Holy Spirit will help us to take every thought captive to the obedience of Christ Jesus (2 Cor. 10:5). We need to have time with Him and be instructed by His Word in order to counter the worldly and demonic messages that come to darken our understanding.

When we are convinced by His Word and are renewed in our mind, our life will be a reflection of Who He is within us. We are taught in Hebrews (12:2) to keep our eyes fixed on Jesus. Otherwise, we may become like the man who looks in a mirror, and after he has gone away, he immediately forgets what kind of person he was. (James 1:24)

Because we were once of this world and its surroundings are still so familiar to us, it is easy to see the people of earth as our reflection and forget that we are "*new creations*" in Jesus. We can then slip back into mimicking their ways instead of mirroring Jesus to them. When they look at us they should see Him and realize that His ways have replaced ours. In 2 Corinthians 3:18, we are told: "*But we all, with unveiled face beholding as in a mirror the glory of the Lord, are being transformed into the same image from glory to glory, just as from the Lord, the Spirit.*"

His Salvation empowers us to walk no longer as slaves to sin. Our old self was crucified with Him that our body of sin might be done away with (Rom. 6:6). By His continued work of Sanctification, we look to the hope of His finished work manifesting in our flesh, even as His Word has accomplished all things in our spirit, by the power of the One Who is now our Life. "*And we know that the Son of God has come, and has given us understanding, in order that we might know Him Who is true,*

and we are in Him Who is true, in His Son Jesus Christ. This is the true God and eternal life." (1 John 5:20)

We know that "*God is not a man that He should lie*" (Num. 23:19). In 1 Peter 1:3-5 this eternal assurance is given: *"Blessed be the God and Father of our Lord Jesus Christ, who according to His great mercy has caused us to be born again to a living hope through the resurrection of Jesus Christ from the dead, to obtain an inheritance which is imperishable and undefiled and will not fade away, reserved in heaven for you, who are protected by the power of God through faith for a salvation ready to be revealed in the last time."* Will we set our minds to agree with God?

To help us, 2 Peter 1:2-3 offers this Promise in the form of a prayer: "*Grace and peace be multiplied to you in the knowledge of God and of Jesus our Lord; seeing that His divine power has granted to us everything pertaining to life and godliness, through the true knowledge of Him Who called us by His own glory and excellence.*" He has provided all we need.

In the light of this confidence, let us walk in that excellence and in a manner that is worthy of Him. No longer are we to behave as people whose minds are set on the flesh, which can only bring death. As His chosen people our minds are to remain set on the Holy Spirit; and as we live and move and have our being in Him, the fruits of His Presence within us will be evident. "*And the fruit of the Spirit is love, joy, peace, patience, kindness, goodness, faithfulness, gentleness, self-control; against such things there is no law.*" (Gal. 5:22)

What more can we say, but "Yes Lord!" All Glory be His forever! Amen.

Devotion Sixteen

"OUR VERY PRESENT HELP"

"The Lord is my light and my salvation; whom shall I fear? The Lord is the defense of my life; whom shall I dread? When evildoers came upon me to devour my flesh, my adversaries and my enemies, they stumbled and fell. Though a host encamp against me, my heart will not fear; though war arise against me, in spite of this I shall be confident. One thing I have asked from the Lord, that I shall seek: that I may dwell in the house of the Lord all the days of my life, to behold the beauty of the Lord, and to mediate in His temple. For in the day of trouble He will conceal me in His tabernacle; in the secret place of His tent He will hide me; He will lift me up on a rock. And now my head will be lifted up above my enemies around me; and I will offer in His tent sacrifices with shouts of joy; I will sing, yes, I will sing praises to the Lord." **Psalm 27:1-6**

Our God is an Awesome God! His Word is excellent and perfect. His help is very near. Oh, that in our

troubled times we would know more deeply the Glory of His Presence.

In Isaiah 26:4-7, it is written: "*Trust in the Lord forever, for in God the Lord, we have an everlasting Rock. For He has brought low those who dwell on high, the unassailable city; He lays it low, He lays it low to the ground. He casts it to the dust. The foot will trample it, the feet of the afflicted, the steps of the helpless. The way of the righteous is smooth; O Upright One, make the path of the righteous level.*"

He is the Rock upon which we stand; and His Name is Jesus! In Him, we are lifted high above our enemies. "*His work is perfect, for all His ways are just; a God of faithfulness and without injustice, righteous and upright is He.*" (Deut. 32:4)

He is our hiding place. He preserves us from trouble and surrounds us with songs of deliverance (Ps. 32:7). He is the same God that delivered Daniel from the lion's den and equipped David to slay Goliath. He is the Mighty God Who parted the Red Sea and made the way of escape for His people! He is Jesus! (Dan. 6:22, 1 Sam. 17:49, Ex. 14:21)

What comfort and assurance to know that we have a God Who is for us! A compassionate God Who is Lord over all! When the armies of darkness descend upon us, we take refuge in the One Who is our confidence, and we will not fear. In the Glory of His Presence we behold His Beauty, and in our meditation we see only Him. The Light of His Countenance dispels all else.

Paul wrote in Philippians 3:10: "*that I may know Him, and the power of His resurrection.*" The word for "*power*" in this passage is "*Dunamis,*" which means "*a miraculous power or force.*" It is derived from the root word "*Dunamai,*" which translates "*to be able or possible.*" As

it is written: "*For all things are possible with God*" (Mk. 10:27).

By the Power of His Word, He raised Jesus from the dead. And the One Who is the Resurrection now lives in the heart of a believer. He created the entire universe and all that it holds. What, therefore, will be impossible to the one who believes in Him?

And in light of this Truth, we have been called to be a people who walk by faith, not by sight (2 Cor. 5:7). "*Faith is the assurance of things hoped for, the conviction of things not seen*" (Heb. 11:1). Before the answer comes or the miracle is realized, the Author and Perfecter of our faith will help us, as we call on Him. We will then be enabled to walk in the peace and rest that trust in Him guarantees. It is in the faithfulness of His Promises that the Lord is glorified, and the enemy is put to shame. And as we offer up songs of praise and shouts of joy, all heaven rejoices, and our King is exalted!

In light of this confidence, 1 Peter 4:12-13 declares: "*Beloved, do not be surprised at the fiery ordeal among you, which comes upon you for your testing, as though some strange thing were happening to you; but to the degree that you share the sufferings of Christ, keep on rejoicing; so that also at the revelation of His glory, you may rejoice with exultation.*"

The Greek word for "*testing*" is "*peirasmos*" and means: "*a putting to proof, i.e. faith.*" As we stand covered by His Shield of Faith, it is not us but His Word that is being tested through the fiery trials. With Promise keeping assurance, His Word will stand the test of fire and we shall come through as refined gold! And because we "*share*" or as in the Greek "*are partakers with*" His sufferings, we are also the beneficiaries of everything that is held within the Victory His finished work has accomplished. Since we have "*shared*" in His death we also

"*share*" in His Glorious Resurrection. Therefore, we can confidently proclaim: "*For I consider that the sufferings of this present time are not worthy to be compared with the glory that is to be revealed to us.*" (Romans 8:18)

Don't lay aside that assurance, precious saints, for He is faithful to His Word, and He will bring it to pass! Keep your eyes fixed on Jesus and you will see the Victory even before it is manifested. As He is, so it shall be. Amen.

Devotion Seventeen

"THE POWER OF HIS PROMISES"

"Bless the Lord, O my soul; and all that is within me, bless His holy name. Bless the Lord, O my soul, and forget none of His benefits; Who pardons all your iniquities; Who heals all your diseases; Who redeems your life from the pit; Who crowns you with lovingkindness and compassion; Who satisfies your years with good things, so that your youth is renewed like the eagle. The Lord performs righteous deeds, and judgments for all who are oppressed. He made known His ways to Moses, His acts to the sons of Israel. The Lord is compassionate and gracious, slow to anger and abounding in lovingkindness." Psalm 103:1-8

In the midst of turbulent trials and distracting circumstances, it is possible to forget Who our Awesome God is and lose sight of His magnificent Nature. The enemy will always attempt to convince us that the Lord is like him, or us. But by His Word, the Lord has made Himself known and has revealed the Glorious riches of His

Kingdom. A heart that is softened in submission to His Lordship will be abundantly supplied in understanding and revelation.

It is God's greatest desire that we know Him, for without that knowledge man will perish (Hosea 4:6). We are instructed in Hosea 6:6: ***"For I delight in loyalty rather than sacrifice, and in the knowledge of God rather than burnt offerings."*** **If we become double-minded in our perception of God's forever Love for us, we become a storm-tossed people entangled in the dark web of fear and unstable in all our ways. Only in the knowledge of the One Who is Love, and the realization that because of His perfection all things have been accomplished for us, can we enter into true rest and be set free from the fear of punishment. If we still fear sin's penalty, we will not be fully convinced that He is for us.**

Therefore, it is good that we go back for a moment to be reminded of the foundational Truth upon which our faith is based. ***"For God so loved the world, that He gave His only begotten Son, that whoever believes in Him should not perish, but have eternal life."*** **(John 3:16)**

Knowing Jesus in a Covenant relationship provides an anchor that will keep us from being carried away by Satan's devices. Our High Priest sympathizes with our weaknesses (Heb. 4:15) and intercedes for us at the Right Hand of the Father (Rom. 8:34). He is the Holy One Who executes judgment against the enemy's accusations that come to oppress His children. He is the Righteous Savior Who supplies Abundant Life, having pardoned all our iniquities by His shed Blood. ***"By His scourging, we are healed"*** **(Is. 53:5). And as He made known His ways to Moses as he journeyed to the Promised Land, He has made Himself known to us as the Way, the Truth and the Life (John 14:6). While we walk with Him in Salvation's**

journey, He is the same One Who is keeping us in His Love; and He will lead us safely home to the Father.

If we are not living in the fullness of this assurance, or are not completely convinced that in Jesus we have been released from the death of sin's punishment, it may be an indication that we have strayed from His Truth. When we are not living in the peace and confidence of Jesus' perfect work of Atonement on our behalf, it is sure evidence that we have laid down the wondrous expectancy of the manifestation of His Glorious Promises in our life.

John 15:7 promises us that: *"If you abide in Me, and My words abide in you, ask whatever you wish, and it shall be done for you."* If we are not abiding in His Word, what words are we abiding in? Through the world's persuasion, the enemy is constantly bombarding us with demonic information that is masqueraded as wisdom. These carnal motivations stir up much busyness and many distractions. To live the Abundant Life, it is vital to set aside some of our Martha duties and sit at His feet as Mary did to learn more of Him. Has Jesus not said?...... *"Take My yoke upon you, and learn from Me, for I am gentle and humble in heart; and you shall find rest for your souls."* (Matt. 11:29)

Only by being fully convinced by and unshakably settled in His Promises will we be able to withstand all the deceptive words of the enemy when he comes to entice or falsely accuse us. The more we learn of Jesus by His Word, the more confident we will become in the security of His Salvation. Even as our spirits in "*new birth*" reality now abide in Him forever, so shall we see the fruit of this sweet abiding in our flesh man as the Holy Spirit's work of Sanctification continues to have its way.

Oh beloved, the Word of the Lord stands forever (Is. 40:8)! No matter what else is taking place in our lives

or whatever we may feel, think or see, our God remains Good! And every Word He has proclaimed from His mouth is Life and Truth to us! He has placed His loving-kindness and compassion as a crown upon our heads, declaring to our enemy that we no longer belong to the realm of darkness, but that we are now children of the King and heirs to His Kingdom of Love, Light and Life! (James 2:5)

May we continue to be encouragers to one another by the word of our testimony, and prayer warriors on each other's behalf, in steadfast faith. Jesus is Lord and He is faithful to His Word. He is our Victory, and all we will ever need in this life and the one to come.

Take heart, dear ones, and give Him all Praise, Honor and Glory forever! Amen.

Devotion Eighteen

"BELIEVE!"

"And Jesus was going about in all Galilee, teaching in their synagogues, and proclaiming the gospel of the kingdom, and healing every kind of disease and every kind of sickness among the people. And the news about Him went out into all Syria; and they brought to Him all who were ill, taken with various diseases and pains, demoniacs, epileptics, paralytics; and He healed them." **Matthew 4:23-24**

As we consider His marvelous and wondrous Word, I pray that the Lord God will open our understanding and increase our faith by the Power of His Spirit. For it is His will that we be not only hearers, but doers of the Word. (James 1:22)

In the last chapter of the Book of Mark (16:15-18), Jesus gives a powerful command: ***"Go into all the world and preach the gospel to all creation. He who has believed and has been baptized shall be saved; but he who has disbelieved shall be condemned. And these signs will accompany those who have believed: in My name they will cast out demons, they will speak with new tongues; they will pick***

up serpents, and if they drink any deadly poison, it shall not hurt them; they will lay hands on the sick, and they will recover."

And in John 14:12-14, these words of our Savior are recorded: *"Truly, truly, I say to you, he who believes in Me, the works that I do shall he do also; and greater works than these shall he do; because I go to the Father. And whatever you ask in My name, that will I do, that the Father may be glorified in the Son. If you ask Me anything in My name, I will do it."*

To fully grasp the empowerment of these Promises, let us learn from the Son of Man as He related to the Father. In the Matthew 4:23-24 account, the Greek word for "*healing*" (every kind of disease and every kind of sickness among the people) is *"therapeuo."* It means *"to wait upon menially, to adore God, to relieve of disease, cure, heal, and worship."*

The manifestation of the miracles Jesus performed came forth from the position of worship that the Son surrendered to the Father. Jesus was in constant fellowship with His Father and remained in the posture of complete devotion and full reliance upon Him. His ear was continually attentive to the One Who had called Him to the Divine purposes for which He was sent. His life was a living adoration to the Father.

When we look earlier on in chapter 4 of the Matthew account, we find what is at the heart of every attack and temptation Satan brings forth from his realm of darkness. As our eyes are opened in Holy Spirit revelation, our remedy to healing and deliverance is clearly understood. By the Word of God, it is evident that the devil tempted Jesus to move outside His Father's leading and Authority with the hope of breaking the bond of fellowship that held them as One. If he could divide them, the lifeline which empowered the Son of Man while He sojourned on earth

would be severed. But as we read further in Scripture we find that the enemy of the Cross was after much more.

For in Matthew 4:8-9, it is written: ***"Again, the devil took Him to a very high mountain, and showed Him all the kingdoms of the world, and their glory; and he said to Him, 'All these things will I give You, if You fall down and worship me.'"*** **Behind every temptation Satan brings against mankind, whether trials or the lure of prideful ambitions, he is after one thing: our worship!**

The response Jesus gave in verse 10 is a powerful key to our resisting the devil: ***"Begone, Satan! For it is written, 'you shall worship the Lord your God, and serve Him only.'"*** **Verse 11 continues:** ***"Then the devil left Him; and behold, angels came and began to minister to Him."***

Whenever worship is offered to the Father, Life and Power are manifested. It is the conduit through which miracles flow. It is what sends the enemy running and firmly establishes our position in relationship with the One Who is over all and in all. In Romans 12:1, Paul exhorts us: ***"I urge you therefore, brethren, by the mercies of God, to present your bodies a living and holy sacrifice, acceptable to God, which is your spiritual service of worship."***

We relinquish all to Him; He accomplishes all in us. However, we do not offer worship to Him as a means to a gain. No, never. But rather we bow our knee before the Living God as did Shadrach, Meshach and Abednego. For even while facing their furnace experience they proclaimed that they knew the Lord would deliver them, but they would not bow their knee to any other god even if He didn't. Their worship was forever His not because of what they knew He would do, but because of Who He is!

We worship Him because He is Worthy! He is Good! And He is faithful to all His Promises! Where He

has spoken, we can know for certain that He will act. Therefore, we say "not our will, but Thy Will be done" and we can rest in the outcome because we trust that His Way is perfect.

***"Oh, the depth of the riches both of the wisdom and knowledge of God! How unsearchable are His judgments and unfathomable His ways!"* (Rom. 11:33)**

Rejoice today, dear ones, and be glad. Worship Him and be healed; honor Him and be delivered; sing songs of praise and be lifted high above all circumstances. For the Lord our God reigns and He is King over all forever! Amen.

Devotion Nineteen

"HIS LOVE NEVER FAILS"

"For I am convinced that neither death, nor life, nor angels, nor principalities, nor things present, nor things to come, nor powers, nor height, nor depth, nor any other created thing, shall be able to separate us from the love of God, which is in Christ Jesus our Lord." **Romans 8:38-39**

I believe that Paul truly was convinced when inspired by the Holy Spirit to pen these powerful words of Scripture. The question I must pose to myself is "Am I?" Am I truly, fully, and completely convinced that there isn't anything or anyone that can separate me from Him and His unconditional Love for me? Not just that He so Loved the world, but that He so Loved me. This is the foundation of confidence that must be securely laid; for upon the Rock of "*God is for me*" are held the assured Victory and guarantee of all His Promises being "*yes and amen*" on my behalf.

And this same question must be answered by every legitimate child of God. For in 1 Peter 2:4-5, it is written: *"And coming to Him as to a living stone, rejected by men,*

***but choice and precious in the sight of God, you also, as living stones, are being built up as a spiritual house for a holy priesthood, to offer up spiritual sacrifices acceptable to God through Jesus Christ.*"**

If the house of God is being shaken by tribulations, distresses, persecutions and the storms of life, then perhaps each living stone needs to look to which foundation it has been secured. We cannot operate in power and authority as kings and priests in the earth unless we are being held firmly in place by the One Who is Love. The foundation of the world is sinking sand and is comprised of the doctrines of demons disguised as knowledge. But the Word of God - the Living Word - is the Cornerstone of our faith and a sure foundation. The wise man or woman who builds upon it shall not fall or fail. A convinced child of God will stand firm no matter what may try to bring him down.

Beloved, please know today that you are loved passionately by the God of all Creation. Trust that Love. It will cast out all fear, because Love has covered a multitude of sins and removed punishment far from us. His Love never fails! If you are feeling shaky or insecure, check your foundation and be sure you are building on Him. If repositioning is required, the Holy Spirit has been given to help us in time of need. He is the mortar that holds all things together. His gift of repentance clears our conscience and allows us to recognize our true identity in Him.

So let us press on, being tightly fitted together in Him in Victory. Let us march on in the Power of His Glory as a house that is not divided, but one in spirit, mind, heart and purpose. And as one voice we shall praise His Name forever! Amen.

Devotion Twenty

"THE DIVINE NATURE"

"Grace and peace be multiplied to you in the knowledge of God and of Jesus our Lord; seeing that His divine power has granted to us everything pertaining to life and godliness, through the true knowledge of Him who called us by His own glory and excellence. For by these He has granted to us His precious and magnificent promises, in order that by them you might become partakers of the divine nature, having escaped the corruption that is in the world by lust." **2 Peter 1:2-4**

Before we go on, please read this awesome Scripture again. Take your time and ask the Holy Spirit for wisdom and understanding because it is so vital that we take hold of this marvelous revelation. As it comes alive in us, it will empower us to live the holy life to which we have been called. But it must come through the "true" knowledge of Him who calls. Settle that issue first. Be sure you are a legitimate child of God. Search your heart. Do you really know Him? Does He really know you? Have you genuinely repented of your sins and surrendered to

the Lordship of Jesus? Have you transcended beyond religious attitudes, opinions or dictates and entered into a personal relationship with the Lover of your soul? Romans 8:16 declares that *"The Spirit Himself bears witness with our spirit that we are children of God."* If you are not, He will show you the Way and lead you into Eternal Life. Once He confirms that you are truly His, stand firm in your identification as His legitimate child.

As His children, we have inherited His precious Promises. By them we have become partakers of His Divine Nature and are now equipped with God's Dunamis Power. Ponder that and rejoice! Believe it and be victorious! We have been made free by the Living Word for *"he who the Son makes free is free indeed"* (John 8:36). A way of escape from the corruption that is in the world has been made for us. *Webster's Dictionary* defines "*corruption*" in part as "*a departure from what is pure or correct.*" If we follow in His footsteps we will not veer off the path of righteousness; for as He is pure so have we been made pure in Him.

By the Sanctifying work of the Holy Spirit, we are being conformed to His Holiness. His Word shapes and corrects us and enables us to live in our new identity. Our flesh man is being aligned with the finished work of Sanctification in our spirit man. To "*sanctify*" means "*to make holy.*" Jesus prayed to the Father for us in John 17:17: *"sanctify them in the truth; Thy Word is truth."* And 1 Peter 1:15-16 commands us: *"but like the Holy One who called you, be holy yourselves also in all your behavior; because it is written, YOU SHALL BE HOLY FOR I AM HOLY."* (Emphasis NASB)

As His body, we are being called to a higher level. He is calling us back from our unbelief, apathy, backsliding and disobedience to once again being a people of "Excellence." As His "*born again*" children, we are to

reflect His image and Divine Nature to the world. And as His Word has already confirmed, we have been empowered to do so and all the more as His Return draws near. The enemy can no longer enslave or control us for he has no part in us. But we must know and remember who we are because of "Whose" we are.

The Glory of the Lord is about to explode within His Church, and we are being readied to experience Him in a greater dimension than ever before. He has sent His "*Refiner's Fire*" and beckons us to willingly step into His cleansing Presence. For to those who will enter in as a living sacrifice (Rom. 12:1), He will burn up everything that is not like Him and catch what remains ablaze. Then as His ministers, we will be sent out as flames of fire and the enemy will be as ashes under our feet. (Heb. 1:7, Mal. 4:3)

Praise Him, and be glad! Remain confident and steadfast in Him and keep pressing on in the true knowledge of Him. The best and most blessed days for the Church are just ahead of us for He comes quickly. Hallelujah!

Devotion Twenty-one

"I AM WHO I AM"

"I am the resurrection and the life; he who believes in Me shall live even if he dies, and everyone who lives and believes in Me shall never die. Do you believe this?" John 11:25-26

When Moses asked God who shall I say has sent me, God answered and said: *"I AM WHO I AM; thus you shall say to the sons of Israel, I AM has sent me to you."* (Exodus 3:14-15)

The Living God revealed Himself as *"Jehovah"* (YHWH) the *"Self-existent One."* It was and is His Covenant Name; it is His Name of Promise. He is Who His Name declares. His Name is all Authority, all Power, all Holiness and Majesty. His Name is Truth, and it is the Resurrection and the Life. And Jesus is still asking: "Do we believe this?" His challenge comes to alert us to examine who and what we believe, for our victory or defeat rests on the foundation of this decision.

Scripture confirms that as His legitimate children, we are the chosen ones who are called by His Name, born of His Name, and sealed by His Name. A name carries

with it an inheritance. However, an inheritance cannot be appropriated unless there is first a death.

Jesus Christ, the great I AM, provided the inheritance requirement on the Cross and then sealed its guarantee by His Glorious Resurrection. He fulfilled every Covenant stipulation to perfection. We are thereby granted the confidence that our inheritance is assured.

All that He is and all that He has is now ours. By way of the true knowledge of Him we are strengthened and lifted high above our circumstances. In sweet meditation let us daily set our minds to remember that:

He is *JEHOVAH-ELOHIM the Lord God, JEHOVAH-ROPHE the Lord our Healer, JEHOVAH-JIREH the Lord our Provider, JEHOVAH-NISSI the Lord our Banner, JEHOVAH-M'KADDESH the Lord Who Sanctifies, JEHOVAH-SHALOM the Lord our Peace, JEHOVAH-TSIDKENU the Lord our Righteousness, JEHOVAH-ROHI the Lord our Shepherd, JEHOVAH-SHAMMAH the Lord Who is always there, and JEHOVAH-SABAOTH the Lord of Hosts...He is JESUS!*

Hallelujah and praise His "NAME" forever!

His Name is all Authority. Therefore, whatever you are going through beloved saint of God, I declare to you today, that by the Power of His Name – "*no weapon that has been formed against you shall prosper.*" No matter what the enemy has purposed in his efforts to rob, kill and destroy, in the "*NAME OF JESUS*," you have already been assured the Victory!

Psalm 91:14 promises us: *"Because he has loved Me, therefore I will deliver him; I will set him securely on high, because he has known My Name.*" (Emphasis mine) The Hebrew word for "*known*" in this Scripture is *"Yada."* It is the word that describes a husband's knowing his wife in the Holy consummation of marriage. We not only carry His Name....we are one with His Name!

Remember, when Satan saw the death of Jesus on the Cross, he thought he had won the victory. But what he could not see was what lay just ahead. He could not know, nor could he fathom that just beyond the Cross, the Glorious Resurrection Power of God was ready to explode with Eternal Life! In Jesus, sin and death have been conquered forever!

In the same way, Satan gloats when he beholds the dying of "*self*" in our flesh man (which must take place in the work of Sanctification), and thinks that he has won the victory over us. He forgets it is in our weaknesses that the Strength of God is being perfected; and in his arrogance he is blinded from seeing what lies just ahead! As we decrease and Jesus increases within us, the Glorious Resurrection Power of God is getting ready to explode in and through us in Dunamis empowered Victory with signs and wonders following to the Praise and Glory of God! (Mark 16:15-18)

There is something so awesome that is just ahead for the Church of the Living God. Keep your eyes fixed on Jesus beloved, stay grounded in His Word and believe in His Name. And there is nothing, absolutely nothing you will not be able to do in that wonderful and very excellent Name!

Devotion Twenty-two

"STAY POSITIONED IN THE LIGHT"

"And this is the message we have heard from Him and announce to you, that God is light, and in Him there is no darkness at all. If we say that we have fellowship with Him and yet walk in the darkness, we lie and do not practice the truth; but if we walk in the light as He Himself is in the light, we have fellowship with one another, and the blood of Jesus His Son cleanses us from all sin." **1 John 1:5-7**

To fully comprehend this Word of Truth, we must go back to the beginning. In Genesis 1:1, it is written: ***"In the beginning God created the heavens and the earth. And the earth was formless and void, and darkness was over the surface of the deep; and the Spirit of God was moving over the surface of the waters. Then God said, 'Let there be light'; and there was light. And God saw that the light was good; and God separated the light from the darkness."***

The Hebrew word for light is ***"owr."*** **It signifies life in contrast to death and brings illumination and enlightenment, which bears the fruits of well being. It is the**

breeding ground from which true joy springs forth. The Hebrew word for darkness is *"choshek"* and means: *"misery, falsehood, ignorance, blindness, that which is hidden, and judgment."* Sin finds its habitat here and breeds every evil thought and action.

Now when God saw that the light was good, He separated the light from the darkness. The Hebrew word for "*separate*" is *"badal,"* which means *"to separate, disjoin, to distinguish diverse things, to discern, make a difference, and to select out of a group."* In doing so, the Living God was revealing His Holiness but was also making a clear line of demarcation within a set standard that was yet to come. His Covenant of Salvation would define the positioning of the people of earth as either those who would remain in the darkness of sin and death, in contrast to those who would be transferred into His Glorious Kingdom of Light and Life. In the Messiah of God the people of Light would become partakers of His Holiness. And in Sacred "*type*" we bear witness to this reality for to be "*Holy"* (Heb. "*qadash"*) is *"to be set apart or consecrated."*

This all falls into place as we read 2 Corinthians 6:14-18: *"Do not be bound together with unbelievers; for what partnership have righteousness and lawlessness, or what fellowship has light with darkness? Or what harmony has Christ with Belial, or what has a believer in common with an unbeliever? Or what agreement has the temple of God with idols? For we are the temple of the living God; just as God said, 'I will dwell in them and walk among them; and I will be their God, and they shall be My people.' Therefore, COME OUT FROM THEIR MIDST AND BE SEPARATE, says the Lord. AND DO NOT TOUCH WHAT IS UNCLEAN; and I will welcome you. And I will be a Father to you and you shall be sons and daughters to Me, says the Lord Almighty."* (Emphasis NASB)

By His Word, the Holy Spirit is speaking to us with Sacred exhortation. His children are holy and precious in His sight. We are Blood-bought and have been washed clean in the Living Water of His Word. He calls to His own to be set apart from the world and the mindset of those who have no dawn (Is. 8:20). His Spirit draws us to come out from practicing their futile ways and to stop running to the vain things that provide no real help in time of need. We must set our minds to not pay attention to doctrines of demons that mask themselves as wisdom. These counterfeits only encourage unbelief against those things the Word has already deemed to be Truth. Even as He separated the light from the darkness in the beginning, so He has separated us as His Light on this earth from the darkness in which the enemy breeds his works of death and destruction.

We are encouraged in John 8:12 that "*he who follows Me shall not walk in darkness, but shall have the light of life.*" His Word is so Awesome! He comes to help and equip us to walk in the Victory that He has already won. The Holy Spirit strengthens us and leads us back to the Way if ever we should go astray. Through Him, we are enabled to see and understand that we are true reflections of the One Who is the pure Light. In Him, we are called to bring illumination and enlightenment to a world that has been darkened in their understanding by the father of lies.

The Sanctifying work of separation is heightening. Remember, to whom much is given, much is required (Luke 12:48). The dividing line drawn from God's Hand is sharp and clear. What the enemy has attempted to blur is being calibrated to distinguish without question — Light from darkness, sheep from goats, wheat from tares, relationship from religion, loyalty from legalism.

The Glory of God is about to be revealed as never before because He comes quickly. Much is at stake, and positioning is critical. To be in Christ, and He in us, is the only hope of Glory. Scripture gives these confirmations: *"If you abide in My word, then you are truly disciples of Mine; and you shall know the truth, and the truth shall make you free"* (John 8:31-32). And in John 15:7: *"If you abide in Me, and My words abide in you, ask whatever you wish, and it shall be done for you."*

If you are His beloved, rest in that assurance and come into full agreement with His Word. Then walk and live in that confidence. If you are not His, run quickly to Him with a heart of repentance and submit to the One Who will grant you Eternal Life in Jesus.

His Bride is being readied. Our gown shines brilliantly with the Shekinah Glory of His Righteousness, and we have been set apart for Him and Him alone. He calls out: "*Be faithful, be true, for you represent Me in the earth and I am longing* to *reveal My Beloved to all creation. My heart yearns to proclaim the victorious cry of* '*Behold My Bride who will reign with Me forever!'* "

Keep looking to Him in all things precious one. His Word gives us this Promise in the form of a prayer: *"Now may the God of peace Himself sanctify you entirely; and may your spirit and soul and body be preserved complete, without blame at the coming of our Lord Jesus Christ. Faithful is He who calls you, and He also will bring it to pass"* (1 Thess. 5:23-24). This assurance will guard us from operating in the dead works of our flesh. The Holy Spirit alone, by His Holy work of Sanctification in us, will bring to completion all He promised concerning us. Therefore, cease striving and know that He is God. He will do it; for in reality, in Him, it has already been done! All He asks for is full surrender from our hearts and

complete trust in His Love. He will carry us to Glory on the wings of His finished work.

It is all about Him. It always has been, and it always will be. Set your mind on His Truth and rest in the Promise of His faithfulness. If the darkness has pressed in on you, fear not. The Light that is in you is greater than the darkness that is in the world. Just believe God, and shine! The darkness will flee away. In the Presence of that Light, the joy and peace you thought had forever eluded you will manifest as when the dawn breaks forth and commands the night to retreat into its hiding place. For in His Presence is the fullness of Joy, Life and Blessing! Then you will be able to fully appropriate the Promise of 2 Corinthians 4:6: *"For God, Who said, 'Light shall shine out of darkness,' is the One Who has shone in our hearts to give the light of the knowledge of the glory of God in the face of Christ."*

Believe it, receive it and share it. Amen!

Devotion Twenty-three

"BEWARE OF A DIFFERENT GOSPEL"

"Grace to you and peace from God our Father, and the Lord Jesus Christ, who gave Himself for our sins, that He might deliver us out of this present evil age, according to the will of our God and Father, to whom be the glory forevermore. Amen. I am amazed that you are so quickly deserting Him Who called you by the grace of Christ, for a different gospel; which is really not another; only there are some who are disturbing you, and want to distort the gospel of Christ. But even though we, or an angel from heaven, should preach to you a gospel contrary to that which we have preached to you, let him be accursed." **Galatians 1:3-8**

It is especially critical in this hour on earth that we fully understand, accept, and preach the true Gospel of Jesus Christ; for it is the unshakable foundation upon which genuine Salvation is held.

By way of the unadulterated Word of Truth, John 3:16 powerfully proclaims: "*For God so loved the world,*

that He gave His only begotten Son, that whoever believes in Him should not perish, but have eternal life."

Mark 1:14-15 also declares: "*And after John had been taken into custody, Jesus came into Galilee, preaching the gospel of God, and saying, 'The time is fulfilled, and the Kingdom of God is at hand; repent and believe in the gospel.'"*

And in John 6:39-40, it is written: "*And this is the will of Him Who sent Me, that of all that He has given Me I lose nothing, but raise it up on the last day. For this is the will of My Father, that everyone who beholds the Son and believes in Him, may have eternal life; and I Myself will raise him up on the last day."*

These Sacred Scriptures convey the heart of the true Gospel of Jesus Christ. God so Loved, God so Gave and God so Saved. And His Voice is still crying out: "*repent and believe!*"

In the Book of Galatians, Paul emphatically warns of a different gospel that was being preached. Judaizers were attempting to bring the Galatian church back into bondage under the Law. They were distorting the true Gospel of Jesus Christ, and by doing so, they were denying the Grace of God that had provided so great a Salvation. However, he also offers other important contrasts: man's reasoning versus God's Revelation, death's curse versus Eternal Life, the vain works of the flesh versus the finished work of Christ, being slaves to sin rather than servants of Jesus, and the liberality of the carnal man versus true freedom as sons and daughters of the Most High God.

As we study line upon line and precept upon precept, we are instructed and warned. We must be careful that we do not succumb to the same deception to which the Galatians were falling prey.

What gospel is being embraced today? Is it truly the Word of Truth that beseeches a lost and dying people to repent of their sins and come into the safety net of Redemption's Promise? Does it preach man's need of the shed Blood of Jesus Christ? Does it magnify the Victory accomplished in His death and Glorious Resurrection? Is it a calling out to be Saved and become separate from this perverse generation? Does it beckon a person to leave the vanities of the world and enter into the Majestic Kingdom of God? Is there recognition of man's hopeless and helpless condition because of the penalty of sin which is death? Is it understood that only the Messiah and Savior of the world, Lord Jesus the Christ, could adequately Atone for and provide acquittal for the punishment that humanity deserves because *"all have sinned and fallen short of the glory of God?"* (Rom. 3:23)

Or is it an enticement to join another version of the world with a "*Christian*" flavor? Does it encourage people to come for what they can get (i.e. wealth, position, and success) or does it demand an acknowledgement of their need of the One Who calls them? Is Jesus being presented as the Holy and Awesome God Who, though He calls us friend, is still the King of kings and Lord of lords? If the questions seem hard, it is only because of the fierceness of the Love Who asks them. Man's responses to these Holy inquiries are critically important; for Eternal Life and death hang in the balance of his answers.

The Father saw the need of mankind being so desperate that He gave His Only Begotten Son, the Precious Son of His heart, to suffer and die an excruciating death to pay the penalty for sin and its consequences. Should we not then understand the urgency of the time, and the great necessity to come back to proclaiming and living the true Gospel of Jesus Christ?

The god of this world preaches a false doctrine of liberality masked as freedom. In reality, he has captivated unsaved man in such an insidious bondage to lust, fear and arrogant pride. Flesh becomes the prison that holds every man and woman who does not have the hope of Jesus in their hearts, in the vanity of the bare and temporal existence of useless expectations. The vessel that will once again return to dust becomes an instrument in the hands of a cruel master whose appetite is insatiable in his demands for control.

While the flesh dies a little more each day, the spirit spirals toward the second death, which will bring eternal torment and separation from the One True God. And though Satan allows his victims to think they are making their own decisions to do what they deem to be right in their own eyes (Judges 21:25), he holds them as puppets on his string of falsehood. The actions of unredeemed man continue to be manipulated and controlled by his own fallen nature. The only way of escape is the miracle of "*new birth*" by which man, in Resurrection Power, is restored to *"oneness"* with the Father.

Man cannot simply become a better version of himself; he must be conformed into the image of the One True God. Regeneration must take place, and repositioning is mandatory. The necessary transfer is from death into Life and darkness into Light. All that is needed has been provided. Jesus said: "*It is finished!*" (John 19:30). He alone is the Way, and the Truth and the Life (John 14:6)! And only in Him is Salvation's safety guaranteed.

The Lord God is raising up His last-day's prophets and ministers who will "*contend earnestly for the faith which was once for all delivered to the saints*" (Jude 1:3). And the Holy Spirit is beckoning: "*He who has an ear, let him hear what the Spirit says to the churches.*" (Rev. 3:13)

The Father, Son and Holy Spirit cry: "*Come!*" Love, Grace and Mercy cry: "*Come!*" The Blood cries: "*Come!*" The angelic hosts cry: "*Come!*" Come out from the world and all its deadly deceptions, and come into the safe haven of the Living Word. Wisdom and Truth light the Way, and Eternal Life awaits with welcoming arms. ***"Come," oh do please "Come!"***

For He is coming soon! Hallelujah & Amen!

Devotion Twenty-four

"REMAIN STEADFAST IN HIS TRUTH"

"As you therefore have received Christ Jesus the Lord, so walk in Him, having been firmly rooted and now being built up in Him and established in your faith, just as you were instructed, and overflowing with gratitude. See to it that no one takes you captive through philosophy and empty deception, according to the tradition of men, according to the elementary principles of the world, rather than according to Christ. For in Him all the fullness of Deity dwells in bodily form, and in Him you have been made complete, and He is the head over all rule and authority." **Colossians 2:6-10**

Now more than ever the battle between Truth and falsehood rages. Many voices are heard throughout the earth, as doctrines of demons are spewed out of the mouths of Satan's ministers. Within their hearts the lies of antichrist are enthroned. They speak words that on the surface sound as though they hold wisdom and help,

but they are only roadmaps that lead further away from the path to Eternal Life.

Many saints are weary, confused and disheartened. Their hearts are steadfast, but a tug of war ensues within their souls. Much is happening within our midst that bears the fingerprints of the Laodicea Church age. In addition, leaders who have been revered as spiritually grounded in integrity are being exposed in deeds of unrighteousness. As the battle continues, doubts beat against the minds of the people of God like stormy waves against a lighthouse.

In the midst of this spiritual war many of God's children cry out: "What is going on, Father? We believe, Lord; please help us understand!" And yet why are we surprised at this fiery ordeal? In Daniel 12:10, it was prophesied that a time would come and is even here, when "*many will be purged, purified and refined; but the wicked will act wickedly, and none of the wicked will understand, but those who have insight will understand.*"

The Hebrew word for "*insight*" is "*sakal*" and means: "*the capacity to act purposely, to have understanding, to pay attention and turn the mind to.*" By its very definition, we are taught that insight involves more than just a mindset or agreement. It denotes action and living participation in what we believe, as revealed in the Light of God's Wisdom and Truth. "*As a man thinks within himself, so he is*" (Prov. 23:7). That is why our God instructs us by His Word in Romans 12:2: "*And do not be conformed to this world, but be transformed by the renewing of your mind, that you may prove what the will of God is, that which is good and acceptable and perfect.*"

***Webster's* definition of "*transform*" is "*to change the nature, function, or condition of.*" We must turn our minds away from the philosophy and empty deceit of the basic principles of the world that have crept into the**

Church. It is imperative that we concentrate on those things that have been revealed and proven by the One Who is the Promise because we become conformed to the very thing we believe. Our natures are transformed by His Word, enabling us to function as the "*new creations*" we are in Him. As we believe God, we are made more into His image and our actions mirror His.

Likewise in Colossians (2:6), we are enlightened that as we have received Christ Jesus, we are to walk in Him. It does not say to walk "*along side of*" but rather "*in*" Him. Jesus Christ is the Living Word. Therefore, we are to walk "*in*" His Word. In Him dwells the fullness of all Power and Authority and we are complete in Him!

So, what should be impossible for us? What should be too difficult? Where can we possibly lack? All confusion, discouragement and darkness scatter like roaches in the Light of God's Promises. Everything becomes clear to us in wisdom and understanding when seen through spiritual eyes. Insight enables us to see into the heart of the matter rather than looking with natural sight superficially. Truth provides 20/20 vision in the Spirit. His Light shines upon and exposes all falsehood, therefore, we can live victoriously because the Living Word has accomplished everything for us and has made all things known to us by His Spirit. No matter what has come against us or how convincing the words of the world can sound, we will live, move and have our being in Him in Victory and Power!

He has given us the assurance that nothing the enemy has purposed will be successful against a legitimate child of God. Walking in the Living Word insulates us from all the schemes of Satan. Our Abba Father guards over us with jealous protection, providing a barrier that cannot be penetrated by any force, weapon or falsehood. Principalities shudder and flee at His Presence. Therefore,

we are safe in Him! We are victorious in Him! We are powerful in Him! We will not be shaken when storms come or things happen that are difficult to understand with our natural minds. We must not lean to our own understanding but trust in the Lord with all our hearts. As we acknowledge Him, our ways will be made straight and our footing will remain sure. We will not stumble over obstacles that Satan throws our way.

So then we must not allow anyone to cheat or deceive us with empty and vain words. Rather we must continue to be rooted and built up in Him and established in the Faith. The Holy Spirit is our Teacher and the One Who leads us into all Truth. To know His Word is to know Him. We need to have the roots of our belief system run deep and strong. Then we will not be shaken or moved when the attacks come. All of our trust and hope must remain in His Word, for only His Word can be trusted.

Oh beloved, read His Word, love His Word, and live His Word! Reverence His Holy Name and worship His Majesty! And be thankful for all He has done. Thank Him for His shed Blood, His suffering, death and Glorious Resurrection. He did it all to Save us from the wages of sin, which is death, and to grant us Eternal Life with Him. A thankful heart creates the atmosphere for abundant living in the midst of any adversity.

And, finally, praise Him in all things. For truly He is Worthy! In Him, we are victorious and have need of nothing. But above all, praise Him for Who He is because He is so Wonderful and so Awesome and He deserves all of our praise forever.

Hallelujah and Amen!

Devotion Twenty-five

"VALLEY OF THE SHADOW OF DEATH"

"Even though I walk through the valley of the shadow of death, I fear no evil; for Thou art with me; Thy rod and Thy staff they comfort me." **Psalm 23:4**

Most people are accustomed to hearing this Scripture read at funerals. It has come to be associated with the passing of a person from the natural realm of his flesh, while living on this planet, to the realm of the spirit world after he dies. However, the truest meaning of this awesome Word addresses a particular state of being in the right here and now.

When David said he would fear no evil, he was describing the struggles and trials he was experiencing while on this earth. The Hebrew word for "*evil*" is "*Ra*" meaning "*a wrong, a moral deficiency, mischief, misfortune, adversity, a bad thing which someone does, a calamity which happens to someone*" and so on. It is derived from the root word "*Ra'a,*" which carries a broad range of meaning designating painful physical or emotional expe-

riences. In the moral realm, it denotes any activity which is contrary to God's Will.

Therefore, it is understood that David could not have been referring to experiences encountered in the after-life. Jesus brings clarity to this revelation in Matthew 4:15-16. Quoting the Prophet Isaiah, He reveals Himself as the fulfillment of Isaiah's prophesy (Is. 9:2): ***"THE LAND OF ZEBULUN AND THE LAND OF NAPHTALI, BY THE WAY OF THE SEA, BEYOND THE JORDAN, GALILEE OF THE GENTILES – THE PEOPLE WHO WERE SITTING IN DARKNESS SAW A GREAT LIGHT, AND TO THOSE WHO WERE SITTING IN THE LAND AND SHADOW OF DEATH, UPON THEM A LIGHT DAWNED."*** **(Emphasis NASB)**

The valley of the shadow of death is this world's system, which is populated by a people who are dead in their trespasses and sins. Jesus Christ, the Light of the world, came to this darkness to show the way of escape from death unto Life. In Ephesians 2:1-10, it is written: ***"And you were dead in your trespasses and sins, in which you formerly walked according to the course of this world, according to the prince of the power of the air, of the spirit that is now working in the sons of disobedience. Among them we too all formerly lived in the lusts of our flesh, indulging the desires of the flesh and of the mind, and were by nature children of wrath, even as the rest. But God, being rich in mercy, because of His great love with which He loved us, even when we were dead in our transgressions, made us alive together with Christ (by grace you have been saved), and raised us up with Him, and seated us with Him in the heavenly places, in Christ Jesus, in order that in the ages to come He might show the surpassing riches of His grace in kindness toward us in Christ Jesus."***

Besides "Hallelujah!" what do we say to these things? If you are a ***"born again"*** **child of God who has been Blood-bought and redeemed in Jesus Christ the Savior,**

you need never fear evil! Although your feet still tread the valley of the shadow of death, God says don't be afraid! I AM with you! The Great I AM is there to manifest everything you need in every situation!

David knew His God. He knew Him to be a God of faithfulness and integrity. David also had understanding of the provision he had in God, thereby saying in Psalm 23:4: *"Thy rod and Thy staff, they comfort me."*

The Hebrew word for *"rod"* is *"shebet."* In the lesser sense, it means a branch or stick. But it also represents the scepter of a king. The rod was a symbol of authority in the hands of a ruler. So, David was in effect saying: "No matter what evil comes near to harm me, Your Word oh God is the Rod of Authority that is over all that concerns me. Your Word is the final word. Evil strategies may have been planned against me, but by Your Word I am delivered, I am healed, and I am made whole." Because David knew that the Living Word of God is the Great I AM, and that He is everything David would ever need, he refused to be afraid. By the Power of His Word, God's Hand of Authority was extended on David's behalf before his enemies. They, therefore, would have to bow their knee to Him!

In further enlightenment, the Hebrew word for *"staff"* is *"misheneth"* and is derived from the root word *"sha'an,"* which means *"to rest upon, to rely on."* Its expounded meaning is *"to place one's confidence on someone or something."* The idiom is *"to lean upon someone's hand."* Therefore, David was confessing to God that because he knew he could trust the Word of Authority that the Lord would send forth on his behalf, he would be able to rest on the Promise of what His Word had assured him. He was in essence saying: "I'll lean on the Hand of Your Authority, Lord, and it will hold me up and keep me safe because my confidence is in You."

Oh beloved, the Lord our God says to you also, "FEAR NOT." Though you may walk through the valley of the shadow of death, be not afraid of any evil. You might pick up some of the dust of that death as you walk earth's way, but the Living Water will wash, refresh and restore you. And His Authority will keep you. God is with you! He is for you! Believe His Promises. Lean and rest on them.

And may all Glory, Praise and Honor be His forever! Amen!

Devotion Twenty-six

"REST IN HIS WORKS"

"For by grace you have been saved through faith; and that not of yourselves, it is the gift of God; not as a result of works, that no one should boast. For we are His workmanship, created in Christ Jesus for good works, which God prepared beforehand, that we should walk in them." Ephesians 2:8-10

In his inherent unredeemed nature, man resides in the tendency of "I will." This innate drive was birthed from Satan's womb of pride and has driven mankind from its inception. The unrest it produces is only matched by the deadness of the works that emanate from man's striving. None of his orchestrated deeds will be adequate to satisfy a Perfect and Holy God. Even in man's boasting, his falling short of that perfection forces him to raise the bar even higher. The greater the heights he attains, the more driven he becomes. But to determine the quality of his work, it must be tested. And God has set the standard; all works will be tested by "Fire."

We are told by the Word of Truth, that as God's children, we have been created for good works. The Word of

God has been implanted in us as seed that He desires to bring forth and reproduce. God is Life. It is through faith in Him that the works of God are birthed. In the Book of John Chapter 6, verses 27-29 it is written: "*Do not work for the food which perishes, but for the food which endures to eternal life, which the Son of Man shall give to you, for on Him the Father, even God, has set His seal." They said therefore to Him, "What shall we do, that we may work the works of God?" Jesus answered and said to them, "This is the work of God, that you believe in Him whom He has sent.*"

The word "*believe*" is derived from the root word "*pistis*," which is the same word for "*faith*." It means to be persuaded by the knowledge of and confidence in the Word of Truth. Our belief in Who God is enriches the soil in the field of our heart into which the seed of His Word in implanted. Out of the abundance of that convinced heart, our mouth speaks the Word of Life. Through this declaration of faith, the works that God prepared beforehand are manifested.

Just as we could not save ourselves, neither can we produce any good work from our own efforts that will please the Lord in any way. It is in the place of Sabbath Rest that we are most productive. Yoked to Him, we simply move in the flow of His creative Power. We are the privileged participants of His finished work and are living out the manifestation of those things He prepared before the foundation of the world. We find the assurance of this heavenly repose in the words of Jesus in Matthew 11:28-30: "*Come to Me, all who are weary and heavy-laden, and I will give you rest. Take My yoke upon you, and learn from Me, for I am gentle and humble in heart; and you shall find rest for your souls. For My yoke is easy, and My load is light."*

Beloved, let us enter into that place of rest where we cease striving and know that He is God! The more we trust in what He has already done, the more we will see those things that bring glory to His Name reflected in our lives.

Praise His Name forever, saints of the Most High God; for truly He is Worthy! Amen.

Devotion Twenty-seven

"STAND!"

"Therefore, take up the full armor of God, that you may be able to resist in the evil day, and having done everything, to stand firm." Ephesians 6:13

By way of *Studylight's Greek Lexicon*, the Greek word for "*stand*" in this passage of Scripture is "*histemi.*" It sets forth the idea of military formation, and by definition, it offers an enlightening understanding of confident positioning. Some of its meanings are as follows: *"to make firm, fix or establish; to uphold or sustain authority, to be kept intact; to be immovable, remain on a sure foundation; to be of a steadfast mind, to stand ready and prepared, to not waiver or hesitate."*

But to fully appropriate the empowerment of this instructional word, we must understand the connection between "*having done everything*" and *"to stand."* In Ephesians 6:11, we read: "*Put on the full armor of God that you may be able to stand firm against the schemes of the devil.*" The ability to stand is provided within the covering of God's Heavenly Armor; and Jesus Christ is that Armor!

If, by faith, you have entered into the Promise of His Salvation, you are "*born again*" of His Spirit and have already done everything you need to do. By the repentance of your sins and heartfelt "yes" to His Lordship, you have been provided with the insulation of Eternal assurance in your Savior. No matter what attacks the enemy may bring, you are safe and victorious because you are hidden in Christ. The Word of God has provided an impenetrable wall of Truth that the devil cannot break through. This knowledge enables us to take a stand in confidence and without fear, because we trust the One in Whom we live, move and have our being.

Look at the weaponry Paul mentions in Ephesians 6:13-17, which will confirm that Jesus is indeed our Armor. The first piece is the Belt of Truth. Jesus is the Way, the Truth and the Life! The next piece is the Breastplate of Righteousness, and He is our Righteousness! We are told to shod our feet with the preparation of the Gospel of Peace, and Jesus is our Peace! We are to take up the Shield of Faith, and Jesus is the Author and Finisher of our faith! We are to take the Helmet of Salvation, and Jesus is our Salvation! Finally, we are to take the Sword of the Spirit, which is the Word of God. Jesus is the Living Word!

Paul told us in the Book of Romans (13:14) that we are to "*put on the Lord Jesus Christ.*" In Him, we are equipped to stand strong and unmovable, knowing that the Victory has already been won. Let the words of Isaiah 41:10 encourage and strengthen us:

> ***"Do not fear, for I am with you; do not anxiously look about you, for I am your God. I will strengthen you, surely I will help you, surely I will uphold you with My righteous right hand."***

Dearly beloved, STAND! Do not be moved! Do not waiver! Trust in the Lord with all your heart, and fear not! He will never leave nor forsake you, and you are forever safe in Him.

Hallelujah and Amen!

Devotion Twenty-eight

"NOW I SEE!"

"Surely our griefs He Himself bore, and our sorrows He carried; yet we ourselves esteemed Him stricken, smitten of God, and afflicted. But He was pierced through for our transgressions, He was crushed for our iniquities; the chastening for our well-being fell upon Him, and by His scourging we are healed. All of us like sheep have gone astray, each of us has turned to his own way; but the Lord has caused the iniquity of us all to fall on Him." **Isaiah 53:4-6**

Take a look, beloved, take a deep penetrating look into the heart of these Living words; for this is Love revealed. Let the Holy Spirit take you back to that moment when Heaven and earth bowed their knees in Holy adoration, and time held its breath in heart-stopping wonderment. Angels looked on with awe and Sacred reverence as Jesus Christ, the Son of God, the King of Glory, the Great I AM, the First and the Last, was stricken, smitten of God, crushed and afflicted!

The Father asks the question through His Prophet Isaiah: "*Who has believed our message? And to whom*

***has the arm of the Lord been revealed?"* (Is. 53:1) Do you believe? Do you understand?**

Read this passage of Holy Scripture again. Only this time read it with the Holy Spirit's help in revelation. Let comprehension crown your thinking as He makes this Truth come alive to "you."

***"Surely my griefs He Himself bore, and my sorrows He carried. Yet I esteemed Him stricken, smitten of God, and afflicted. But He was pierced through for my transgressions, He was crushed for my iniquities; the chastening for my well-being fell upon Him, and by His scourging I am healed. Like all of His sheep, I have gone astray, and have turned to my own way; but the Lord has caused my iniquity to fall on Him."* (Emphasis mine)**

Now can you see? Now do you understand? He did it for you!

When Light comes, blindness must give way to sight. Job came to understand this when he reached the end of himself. In Job 42:5 his words echo his heart's illumination: "*I have heard of Thee by the hearing of the ear; but now my eye sees Thee.*" What he had confessed by faith, he could now see in reality. "*For I know that My Redeemer lives.*" (Job 19:25)

Beloved, Jesus the Living Word and Creator of the entire universe, conquered sin and death forever with your name written on His heart! He destroyed all the works of the devil and has provided you with the Victory in whatever you may be facing or going through. You are loved! You are forgiven! You are healed!

Your Good Shepherd is calling you back to the green pasture of His Word.

He beckons you to come, eat and be made full. It is there, in His Glorious Presence, that you will find comfort and rest for your soul. In the rich and fertile ground

of His Promises, you will grow strong in His Strength. Everything you need is in Him – only come!

"Who has believed our message, and to whom has the arm of the Lord been revealed?" **I believe Lord, I believe! For I have heard, I have come, and now I see!**

Hallelujah and Amen.

Devotion Twenty-nine

"HIS HAND IS FOREVER UPON ME"

"Let Thy hand be upon the man of Thy right hand, upon the son of man whom Thou didst make strong for Thyself. Then we shall not turn back from Thee; revive us, and we will call upon Thy name. O Lord God of Hosts, restore us; cause Thy face to shine upon us, and we will be saved." **Psalm 80:17-19**

As the clock in God's prophetic timeline continues to tick quickly toward midnight, we draw closer to the "End of the Age" and the fulfillment of all His Promises that He has made sure by His forever and faithful Word. Knowing his time is short, the enemy's attacks have increased with fervent intent. Therefore, the people of God have been deluged with many trials and circumstances, and many have become weary and battle-torn. In the valley of these weaknesses, the temptation to shrink back looms over God's army. But the Holy Spirit, Who is our Helper, has come with His heavenly aid to tend to your wounds valued soldier of the Most High God. He has come to bring you back to service in His Strength

and Might. It is time to move out of that valley of oppression and press on to Mount Zion!

Every act of righteousness that the Living God performs He does for His Own Namesake and because of Who He is. This gives rest to the child of God and sets us free from the dead works of our own striving. God is not moved by man's personal merits or self-motivated actions. He is moved by His Word.

God is Love. Therefore, His relationship with us does not change by measure of our behavior. He loves us because it is the very Essence of His Nature to do so. His Love is unconditional and it is forever. We need never fear losing it.

And because His Hand is upon us, His Authority is extended on our behalf by His Love, Grace and Mercy. By Him and in Him, we are "*Saved.*" That Sacred work of Salvation continues to manifest His Power as He brings everything concerning us into the completion of His finished Atonement on the Cross.

In Ephesians 1:3-8 we are granted this Eternal assurance: *"Blessed be the God and Father of our Lord Jesus Christ, who has blessed us with every spiritual blessing in the heavenly places in Christ, just as He chose us in Him before the foundation of the world, that we should be holy and blameless before Him. In love He predestined us to adoption as sons through Jesus Christ to Himself, according to the kind intention of His will, to the praise of the glory of His grace, which He freely bestowed on us in the Beloved. In Him we have redemption through His blood, the forgiveness of our trespasses, according to the riches of His grace, which He lavished upon us."*

This confidence is the loving boost that moves us up and out of the failings of our flesh man and enables us to walk by the Spirit of God in Resurrection Power. We live

in the assurance that *"Greater is He Who is in us, than he who is in the world."* (1 John 4:4)

The Holy Spirit bears witness to Himself within our spirit, confirming that we are a legitimate child of God. And it is within this Truth that we are revived. The Greek word for "*revive*" is "*chayah*" and means: "*to live, to enjoy life, to live anew, to recover, to be well, to make alive, to enliven, and to restore to life.*"

If you do not find yourself living out that fullness of Life, beloved, you need only sit down at the banquet table of His Word and partake of His Heavenly Manna! His Promises will nourish and revive you. He will strengthen you in the confidence that you are His child and are precious and much loved by the God of your Salvation. His Hand is upon you to bless you and guide you in the way you should go. It will keep you steadied and set firmly in place and will be the safeguard that keeps you from turning back.

There is a work to be done as we carry out the manifestation of His finished work on earth. You are vital to God in His end-time purposes, therefore, He is with you to revive and restore you to that position of mountain-moving Faith. His Grace has empowered you to speak to those mountains of opposition and bring them crashing down with the echo of "*not by power, nor by might, but by My Spirit says the Lord of Hosts.*" (Zech. 4:6)

Rise up in His Strength, beloved, and press on in Victory. And do please give Him all Praise, Honor and Glory forever!

Devotion Thirty

"LIVING AS A NEW CREATION"

"I urge you therefore, brethren, by the mercies of God, to present your bodies a living and holy sacrifice, acceptable to God, which is your spiritual service of worship. And do not be conformed to this world, but be transformed by the renewing of your mind, that you may prove what the will of God is, that which is good and acceptable and perfect." Romans 12:1-2

When the world looks at the children of God, they should see a difference. Our behavior should reflect Jesus to them in such a way that we become more than just another company of people they have learned to tolerate. To walk in a manner that is worthy of the Lord is offered as living worship before His Throne. What pleasure it gives Him to see His image mirrored in His children. As we are looked upon, it is this family resemblance that separates us from all other people on the earth.

Therefore, we are exhorted to beware of being conformed to this world, but rather we are to be transformed by the renewing of our minds. The Greek word for "*transformed*" is "*metamorphoo*" and is used in Holy Scripture to describe the transfiguration of Jesus. It involves the miracle of transformation from an earthly form into a supernatural, which is denoted by *"radiance."*

The Greek word for "*renewing*" is "*anakainosis*" and means "*qualitatively new, making a person different than what he was in the past.*" At the moment of Salvation, we experienced a transfiguration within our spirit man, whereby old things passed away, and all things became new (2 Cor. 5:17). In that very instance, we were restored to the image of God that had been lost in the Garden of Eden. A *"born again"* child of God shines with the radiance of God Himself as Light into the darkness of the world. We are now "*new creations*" in Him and are no longer children of darkness. We have become children of Life and Light, and in our spirit man are just like our Father.

We cannot be reminded often enough of the "*newness*" that has been appropriated to us in Christ Jesus our Savior. When we let our minds go astray from meditating on this awesome reality, we become darkened in our thinking. We must practice setting our minds and continue to take every thought captive unto the obedience of Christ Jesus (2 Cor. 10:5). Our minds are where Satan wages his greatest strategies. He will bring false accusations against us with the hope of convincing us that we are still that "*old person.*" But if we understand who we now are, because of Who He is within us, our actions will reflect our "*new nature.*" Remember, 2 Peter 1:3-4 assures us that: "*His divine power has granted to us everything pertaining to life and godliness, through the*

true knowledge of Him Who called us by His own glory and excellence. For by these He has granted to us His precious and magnificent promises, in order that by them you might become partakers of the divine nature, having escaped the corruption that is in the world by lust."

No matter how weak we feel or how many times we fail, we must continue to set our minds to agree with God's Word concerning us. He always looks at us through the Blood of Jesus and has given us the Promise that He will bring to completion that good work He has begun in us. (Phil. 1:6)

By the Sanctifying Power of the Holy Spirit, He is perfecting all things as He readies us for His soon Return. As we serve Him in our waiting, it is the Dunamis provision of God within our spirit man that equips us to walk in a manner that is worthy of Him. The more we decrease and He increases within us, the more His power will be evidenced in our lives.

In light of these things, it is a good thing when we can say we have lost "*our*" mind because it has been replaced with the "*Mind of Christ.*" This is the "*renewed mind.*" And this is the good and acceptable and perfect will of God.

Therefore, continue to press on in Him, beloved, and praise His Name forever. For He is forever Worthy!

CPSIA information can be obtained at www.ICGtesting.com
Printed in the USA
LVOW11s0918270815

451701LV00001B/7/P